Quality in School Education

Quality in School Education

Secondary Education and Education Boards

Manju Narula

NUEPA

SHIPRA

(2022 PoD, 2007, First Published 2006)

Rs.1250; US$ 42

ISBN : 978-81-7541-274-3

2024 Impression (PoD)

Quality in School Education:
Secondary Education and Education Boards

Published by:
SHIPRA PUBLICATIONS
LG 18-19, Pankaj Central Market,
I.P. Ext., Patparganj, Delhi 110092
91 11 47322068; 9650028065, 9810522367
info@shiprapublication.com
www.shiprapublication.com

Foreword

Secondary education is poised for a new leap in the near future. This leap would be guided by certain compelling conditions that are part of the social and political framework of the country as well as by concerns of education as an instrument of human development. Having eluded for more than 50 years, it is only now that universal elementary education seems to be within sight. *Sarva Shiksha Abhiyan* has made significant strides and impact on the enrolment of children. Retention is still significantly low; so is the performance of students. Given the trend, the growth in enrolment seen as a social function, there will generate positive pressures for better retention and improved quality, which will get strengthened with the resolve and support of the government and the civil society.

Research provides clear evidence that very large majority of children who survive the first eight years of schooling, transit to the secondary level-more than 85 per cent of them. In NIEPA, we created certain alternative scenarios of secondary education based on the assumed success of SSA. In the most likely scenario, an additional 11 million children will be added to secondary classes by 2010; this is almost 1.5 times of its existing capacity. This quantum shift in the demand for secondary education will also be guided by the social aspirations of people and the growing size of middle class in the country. Then, there is the external compulsion of globalization and global competitiveness of Indian workforce that will determine the quality of products and services. The future scenario of secondary education will be characterized by massive quantitative expansion with strong qualitative changes.

I had the privilege of organizing and chairing a national conference from the platform of NIEPA, 'Focus Secondary Education' in 2001. It is at this conference that for the first time in the country, I raised the 'issue' of 'universal secondary education'. Government of India appointed a CABE Committee in 2005 on universalization of secondary education. The Committee submitted its report, and CABE has approved it. Although there is no firm decision yet, Ministry of Human Resource Development has already initiated the process of including universal secondary education within the planning parameters from the 11th five-year plan. There is a possibility that Government may launch some kind of Madhyamik Shiksha Abhiyan in the pattern of *Sarva Shiksha Abhiyan*.

Universalization of Secondary Education has to be an intensive partnership game of the states and the centre; within the states, among the various state level organizations and institutions, namely the State Directorate of Education, SCERT, State Textbook Bureau, and the all important Boards of Secondary Education. The issue of expansion of-secondary education facilities for ensuring access will be the domain of the State Directorate of Education. The question of quality of education like curriculum framework for the education of the adolescents with multiple intelligence, modernization of curriculum, capacity building of teachers and heads of schools, students' assessment in scholastic and non-scholastic areas and their certification will largely be the domain of activities of the Boards of Secondary Education, particularly since SCERTs in many states have intense engagement with universalization of elementary education. The onus of quality development in secondary education will be on the heads and shoulders of Boards of Secondary Education.

The Boards of Secondary Education has traditionally been associated with examination and certification. This has continued despite the change in their names, though some boards have assumed substantial academic role. The time has come to substantially change their character for the Boards to emerge into academic leadership position in school education in the states.

The Study by Dr. Manju Narula, sponsored by NIEPA comes at the most opportune moment in the history of development of secondary education in India. Her primary focus has been on the academic role of the Boards, particularly, quality management in secondary education. Given the limits of a time bound research by an individual scholar, she managed to study four Boards in the country. There can always be a debate whether four boards can adequately represent the intricacies of as many as 42 Boards of Secondary Education in the country. But then, this study provides an important window to all other states and Boards to look into their own work domain.

In fact, right at this moment, NIEPA is engaged in two other massive national studies-one on delivery of secondary education and the other is on Role of Boards of Secondary Education examining the process of modernization, quality management, management of diversity, management of flexible learning systems and research and development in the Boards of Secondary Education. Though not originally planned, Dr. Manju Narula's study provides creates a 'pilot study' platform for the major national study to draw upon.

I complement and congratulate Dr. Manju Narula for undertaking this study. It is never easy to collect data from Boards that are round the year busy with examination related fire fighting. It is important to appreciate the sensitivities with which Boards of Secondary Education have to work in the country. Yet, they provided all the support that they could manage to the researcher. I feel grateful to Chairpersons and the staff of all the four Boards for their support.

Quality management in secondary education will become a far more increasing and important issue. I hope this study will inspire and encourage other researchers to undertake research in this area and shed light on the mystery of quality in education.

August 12, 2005 **Marmar Mukhopadhyay**
NIEPA, New Delhi

Preface

Secondary education is a crucial and terminal stage of the school education system. It is a gateway for higher education and also a vital link to the world of work. The developed countries have reached a stage where secondary education has become universal; it is undergoing a transformation in the developing countries including India.

In India, the Boards of Secondary Education are responsible for implementing the secondary education system in the country. Accordingly, it is their duty to manage change and quality in schools education in the country. The main challenge before the Boards are that there is a constant threat of knowledge getting obsolete day by day, on the other the requirement for updating the existing facilities remains a financial challenge. The Boards must think constantly about the ways and means to absorb the changes that will soon become necessary.

Over the years, the Boards of Secondary Education have undergone a process of functional change from being examination Boards to Secondary Education Boards and finally to Boards of School Education. This has resulted in many modifications in the working of the Boards. In order to respond to new situations effectively, the functioning of the Boards need to be flexible and dynamic. The Boards need to widen the sphere of their operations and increasingly support schools in undertaking innovative activities and in offering high quality education. They need to adopt several measures, for instance, concerning academic guidance and supervision, preparation of quality teaching-learning material, adoption of progressive modes of evaluating students' performance, training of teachers, principals and other personnel, and evaluation of the performance of schools affiliated to them. In addition, revolutionary advancements in communications technology have broken the national boundaries. As a consequence, globalization has created several avenues and possibilities for educational sector. Therefore, there is exigency to see how Boards of Secondary

Education are prepared for facing these challenges.

The present book is the outcome of a research project sponsored by NIEPA. It deals with the issues of managing change and quality by the Boards of Secondary Education in four states of India i.e, Himachal Pradesh, Madhya Pradesh, West Bengal and Andhra Pradesh. I must express my gratitude to Chairpersons and staff of all the four Boards for providing time as well as relevant information about the Boards.

I owe gratitude to Prof. Marmar Mukhopadhyay, Director NIEPA, who is a guiding spirit behind this study. He is not only inspired me to take up the study but also gave guidance at all the stages of work, which were encouraging enough to complete the study within the stipulated time. I express my sincere thanks to Prof. B.P. Khandelwal Former Director, NIEPA, Prof. Sudesh Mukhopadhyay, Senior Fellow and Head, Policy Unit and Prof. Najma Akhtar, Senior Fellow and Head, Educational Administration Unit for rendering valuable suggestions during this study. My thanks are also due to Shri P.R.R. Nair, Registrar, NIEPA for providing all necessary administrative support to complete the study in-time.

I thank Shri. S.S. Kalra for the meticulous copy-editing of the manuscript. My thanks are due to Mr. Sudhir Dagar for typing the manuscript of this book. He managed data entry and page layout single-handed. I owe my thanks to Shri Pramod Rawat, Deputy Publication Officer and his colleagues, especially Shri. Sudhakar Mishra and Shri. Jai Prakash Dhami of the publication Unit, for rendering necessary assistance in the publication of this book.

I hope that this study will be of value for educational planners, policy makers and researchers. Also it would generate ideas and actions so as to enable our Boards of Secondary Education to meet the future challenges of globalization.

September 15, 2005 **Manju Narula**
NIEPA, New Delhi

Contents

List of Tables and Figures

TABLES

FIGURES

Abbreviations

ACGE	Assistant Commissioners for Government Examinations
AEAs	Advanced Extension Awards
AICSE	All India Council for Secondary Education
ALT	Achievement Level Test
AS	Advanced Subsidiary
BSEAP	Board of Secondary Education, Andhra Pradesh
BSEMP	Board of Secondary Education, Madhya Pradesh
CBSE	Central Board of Secondary Education
CCE	Continuous and comprehensive evaluation
ICSE	Indian School Certificate Examination
COBSE	Council of Boards of School Education
CSE	Certificate of Secondary Education
D.Ed	Diploma in Education
DEO	District Education Officer
DEPSE	Directorate of Extension Programmes for Secondary Education
DPEP	District Primary Education Project
DPI	Director Public Instruction
ETT	Elementary Teacher Training
GCE	General Certificate of Education
GCE O-level	Grade 10
GCE A-level	Grade 12
GATT	General Agreement on Tariffs and Trade
GNVQ	General National Vocational Qualifications
GSCE	General Certificate of Secondary Education
HPSEB	Himachal Pradesh Secondary Education Board
IASE	Institutes of Advanced Studies in Education
ICR	Integrated Computerized Registration
ICT	Information Communication Technology
JBTC	Junior Basic Teachers Certificate
LAN	Local Area Network

MOE	Ministry of Education
MM	Mumtazul Muhammadin
NIEPA	National Institute of Educational Planning and Administration
NCERT	National Council of Educational Research and Training
NIOS	National Institute of Open Schooling
NCC	National Cadet Course
NPE	National Policy on Education
NVQ	National Vocational Qualification
POA	Programme of Action
PPR	Post Publication Review
PPS	Post-Publication Scrutiny
PPTTC	Pre-Primary Teachers Training Certificate
PTC	Pandit Training Courses
PVTC	Physical Education Training Certificate
RMV	Rabindra Mukta Vidyalaya
SCERT	State Council of Educational Research and Training
SSA	Sarve Shiksha Abhiyan
SSC	Secondary School Certificate
SUPW	Socially Useful Productive Work
TTC	Teachers Technical Certificate
UNICEF	United Nations Children Emergency Fund
WBBME	The West Bengal Board of Madrasah Education
WBBSE	West Bengal Board of Secondary Education
WBCHSE	West Bengal Council of Higher Secondary Education
WTO	World Trade Organization

1

Quality in School Education and Role of Education Board

Introduction

School Education plays an important role in the all round development of a child. One of the ways to assess the all round development of a child is examination. The purpose of an examination is to discover whether students have assimilated the expected measure of knowledge and skills as per the prescribed curriculum and whether they have reached an adequate level of attainment in line with the goals of secondary schools. But over the years, examination process deviated from its path and became the means to get certification for entry into higher education. In the context of conducting school examination and issuing certificates, the Board of Secondary Education has a significant role. Therefore, an important area for consideration in secondary education is the role Education Boards play in achieving the quality of secondary education. The success of the Boards depends upon how they cope with the management of change to maintain quality in education.

In India, in the colonial period, the Dispatch of Charles Wood emphasised upon the then Government to pay more attention to higher education than to primary and secondary education. The decentralisation of education was introduced in 1870. It carried certain qualifications, which were relevant from the point of view of the then Government of India's role in Indian education. Though during 1870s, the provinces were given the responsibility of day-to-day administration of education, but by virtue of grant-in-aid, the overall control of educational policy still remained with the Centre. In 1917, in order to devolve authority in education to provinces, the role of

Centre in education was discussed at length and it was decided to set up a permanent Board of Education. As a result, the Board of Secondary Education was established. Its main aim was to safeguard and coordinate standard in education. United Provinces Board of High School and Intermediate Education was the first Board to be set up in 1921. The time came when the Board did not find it possible to shoulder this gigantic responsibility any longer because of enormous enrolment. The Government of the United Provinces requested the then Government of India, that since the Board was not able to maintain an efficient administration in the circumstances, the candidates from areas outside the United Provinces should not be admitted to the Board's examination beyond the year 1927-28. As a result of the representation, the then Government of India decided to set up a joint Board for all the areas. The establishment of the joint Board was accompanied by a rapid growth and expansion of secondary education in the country. The Board did creditable work in enhancing the quality and standard of education in the institutions recognised by it through periodic inspections carried out by inspectors. In 1929, Hartog Committee recommended diversification of curricula in the schools from upper middle stage as universities had dominated the whole secondary education. Again the Sapru Committee, 1934, also recommended diversification of courses to remove large-scale unemployment. The Sargent Report in 1944 came up with the suggestion that high school education should be of six years' duration and it should be of two types: (a) Academic, and (b) Technical.

After independence, an Education Commission (1948-49) was set up to review the university education. The Commission, among other recommendations, also suggested twelve years of schooling at secondary and intermediate stage and referred for urgent reforms. The students on completion of the course were expected to take the final examination, namely high school certificate examination or higher secondary certificate examination. The Secondary Education Commission of 1952-53, commonly known as Mudaliar Commission recommended the establishment of a Board of Secondary Education to deal with all aspects of education at the secondary stage, especially to look into the problem of the lack of validity, reliability and objectivity in examinations and to remove the shortcomings of the examination system. The All India Council for Secondary Education (AICSE) was set up with three basic areas of priority for initiating its work: examination reform, in-service teacher education and science education. The AICSE was renamed in 1959 as the Directorate of Extension Programmes for Secondary Education (DEPSE). The activities of AICSE and DEPSE naturally focused themselves at secondary education. They rejuvenated secondary education through the establishment of Extension Services Departments attached to teacher training colleges, the launch of a massive movement of examination reform, which fast permeated the whole country. In 1964-66 the Education Commission was set up. The Commission had given considerable attention to school education. It advocated that a Board of School Education be established in each state in the country for effective academic control and supervision of examinations and suggested to establish Central Examination Reform Unit in the National Council of Educational Research and Training (NCERT). In 1967, the National Policy on Education postulated establishment of National Board of School Education, which would coordinate at the national level the standards prescribed for attainment by the state Boards of school education. It would make arrangements to evaluate the standards actually attained on a school, district, state and national bases. Some of the National Education Policy plans have been implemented. One of them was the establishment of a Board of school education in each state. And second, establishment of the Central Examination Unit in the National Council of Educational Research and Training, along with the All-India Council for Secondary Education became its part, and has been working vigorously ever since to refine and improve examinations and development of comprehensive programme of examination reform. It aimed to improve written, practical and oral examinations; introduce internal assessment procedures on scientific lines; and bring about consequential changes, as for example, in curriculum and textbooks, etc. Main proposals for the improvement of written examinations comprised (i) improvement of questions and (ii) improvement of question papers. In 2001 NCERT published a manual on how to use grades for admissions. The pros and cons of implementing grading system were given in detail.

The role of the Boards was discussed in the National Policy on Education (NPE), 1986, and the Programme of Action (POA), 1992. The POA has listed some drawbacks, which the system is facing due to excessive examination orientation of school education. The document suggests much wider and larger role to be played by the Boards besides being the examining body.

A few studies have been carried out in India on the functioning of the Boards as well as on reforms. Sharma (1991) provided a unique blend of theoretical perspective and empirical evidence covering three decades. It is a comparative study of the administration of Boards of school education in India with special reference to historical background of secondary education and legal aspects. Based on the functioning of Boards of school education in India, Sharma strongly suggests improvements in the entire examination system at secondary education level and reformation in setups of the Boards. He forwards proposals regarding the day-to-day functioning of the Boards, their administrative and academic aspects. He finds that the Boards have not shown much concern for the personnel, and how best their efforts can be organised to achieve the desired objectives. Also, attempt has been made primarily to systematise and describe the administration of different Boards of school education.

Government in 1997 set up a Task Force on the Role and Status of Boards of Secondary Education under the chairmanship of Prof. Amrik Singh. The Committee did extensive survey of all the Boards and studied the present position and status of Boards of Secondary Education. The Committee suggested restructuring the school Boards and emphasised their academic role rather than performing only examination-oriented activities. In addition, it stressed on autonomous status of the Boards, as it will increase flexibility, diversity of operations, more emphasis on research, in-service training, etc. and above all better accountability. On top the Committee recommended that students should be equipped with requisite amount of knowledge, and skills needed at work, to enable them to become self-employed. It will bring down transition rate from higher secondary stage to college level. This has to be corrected soon by revising the curriculum from time to time and coordination with other concerned groups such as industry, commerce, agriculture, science and technology including information technology.

Tata Consultancy Services (1997) did a study on Organisation Structure of Board of High School and Intermediate Education of Uttar Pradesh. They concluded that poor work-culture, less autonomy in financial matters, lack of deployment of information technology, lack of academic orientation, litigation cases, etc., adversely affected the Board's functioning.

Sudesh Mukhopadhyay (2002) took up a study on 'Enhancing the Academic Role of School Boards of Education'. She organised a

National Meet. The case studies on four School Boards, i.e., Uttar Pradesh, Mizoram, Rajasthan and Maharashtra were presented in this National Meet. In addition, Amrik Singh's study 'Remodelling of School Education Board', was also discussed in the meeting. It was discussed that instead of concentrating only on publication of results more attention was required for its academic role *vis-à-vis* production of materials and textbooks and getting a feedback from the field for improving the functioning of Boards in areas which affect the academic excellence of schools. Mostly, Boards are preoccupied with the examination functions. It showed a concern on the way Boards do justice to all the roles. The study also mentioned that there are many bodies controlling the secondary education. Their functions sometimes overlap with each other. Hence, it is necessary that Boards develop a dialogue with state governments to clearly the designate roles, which would strengthen each other rather than weaken the secondary education. Quality of secondary education would require inputs from all these but in an integrated and cohesive manner.

The Boards of Secondary Education are the main agencies for conducting external examination. Examinations are the backbone of educational system, and play a significant role in determining what goes on in the classroom, what the teacher teaches, how students learn, how much teachers have developed the ability of understanding and critical thinking in students, and how much deep approach the students have adopted in learning. Therefore, examinations support teaching-learning process. But question arises: does it happen? According to Parameswarm (2002) the examination reforms and change have occupied a very prominent position in our scheme of educational reforms and change for more than five decades. We have had committees of experts in this regard but by and large not much of a change has been achieved. The classroom teacher does not yet have a clear appreciation of the philosophy and logic of examinations and evaluations. The paper is intended to familiarise the classroom teachers and others interested in education with some of the issues and problems connected with the design and conduct of examinations. The teachers as well as student are victim of this peculiar system.

Most of the Board publications are only on 'Examination Reform' and convey an impression as if they have been established to conduct and manage only examinations. Seminar organised by Assam Higher Secondary Education Council on 'Examination Reforms' (1997) was attended by many chairmen of education Boards. They by and large stressed on the issues related to quality of question papers, introduction of continuous and comprehensive evaluation, reforms in question papers, teacher training on model question preparation, question bank, methods to check malpractices, etc.

Khandelwal (2003) mentioned in the article futuristic paradigms for Boards of school education. The Boards have to assume a new role for justifying their existence for their sheer survival. The change has however to be well thought out and gradual. The closing in advances of WTO-GATT are some important reason for urgency in this task. In addition switching over various other issues like: improvement of examination mechanisms and management for ensuring accuracy, dependability, justice and credibility of the results, introduction of subject-wise grades, without declaration of students as pass or fail, pursuing a gradual time-bound programme for the certification of performance levels to institutions by strengthening the system of comprehensive and continuous school-based evaluation, review of curriculum in the right sprit and perspective, introduction of large scale programmes of in-service teacher education for up-dating their knowledge of content and up-grading their skills of objective-based teaching, etc.

Gakhar (2004) in an article "Basics of Good School" stressed on five indicators that a school need to have, i.e., curriculum, instructional mechanism, evaluation and assessment, teacher resources, and total infrastructure. Emphasising on these indicators any management team of a school can develop a good school from the existing one. Good schools must create specialised learning programmes for students. Though these may be based broadly on the national curriculum, they should try better and new methods of instruction. One of them can be integrated learning mechanism. In integrated learning mechanism, lessons are a blend across the curriculum, i.e., from different subjects to make learning more interactive, interesting and effective. For example, Music/Art can be used in teaching of Science or English. Good school needs to create its own evaluation and assessment system. Teachers are the nerve system of any school. Therefore, training programmes for teachers on a regular basis to upgrade their knowledge of the system need to be organised.

The backdrop suggests that after the establishment of the first school education Board in UP in 1921, the Boards, over the years have undergone a process of functional change from being Examination Boards to Secondary Education Boards and finally to

Boards of School Education. Earlier there used to be only one Board in a state conducting secondary and senior secondary examinations. Now a large number of states have two Boards, one conducting secondary and the other senior secondary examination. At present, there are 42 Boards/Councils of Higher Secondary Education. There are also three more Boards at the national level—the CBSE, CISCE and NIOS.

Over a period of time, various changes have taken place in education scene. The modifications in organisational structure, administrative policies and programmes subsequent to the implementation of the National Policies on Education (1967 and 1986) and Programme of Action (1992), and reports submitted by state-level education commissions and committees have had effect on the working of the Boards. In addition the paradigm shifts call for more initiatives from the Boards of school education besides improving validity, reliability and objectivity for examinations they conduct for ensuring accuracy, and dependability. The Boards have to invest additional efforts for further improving the management of examinations.

Hence, the questions have been raised regarding the role of the Boards in the context of rapid changes that have been taking place in the education system:

- How these Boards have grown in terms of schools and number of students?
- What are their major strengths and weaknesses?
- Whether they had done any reforms or innovations?
- What is their attitude regarding management of change in the school education?
- What is their role in management of quality in school education?

In this context two issues emerge: one, management of change, and two, how management of change helps in bringing quality in the schools. Management of change is not a new topic. The issue gained importance in 1980s. First of all, to bring any change in the institution a new idea has to be adopted and institutionalised. The process of adoption and institutionalisation passes through installation, trial, adoption, evaluation and internalisation (Rogers, 1962). Two types of factors at the system level and institutional level influence change in the organisations. At the system level, planning skill, incentives, professional support, authority, implementing manpower, bureaucracy etc. affect the change in the institution. At the institutional level, leadership, staff, authority, resources, communication and linkages, nature of innovation, accountability, incentives etc. affect the change (Mukhopadhyay, 1980). According to Robert and Macalman, management of change is a complex, dynamic and challenging process. The successful change depends upon clear and shared vision. Change is never a choice between technological, organisational or people-oriented solutions, but involves combination of integrated strategies designed to produce results. Mukhopadhyay (2001) presents several mechanics of change: (a) one that communicates innovation (resource system); (b) to whom the innovation is communicated for adoption (adopter system); (c) innovation itself; (d) the process through which innovative ideas are transferred (communication). Thus to bring change in an organisation, the institutional level and the system level heads of the institute have a key position. They have to adopt several strategies and take decisions to implement any new idea or to bring change in the organisation.

The Boards of Secondary Education are dealing with improvement of education standard at the secondary level. Therefore, from time to time to bring change in the system, the chairman or the president of the Board has to take certain decisions. The present study looks into how far chairman or president of the Board has been able to cope with changes that came up over the years in secondary education.

Quality has been one of the major concerns of education. In the era of globalisation, quality has become all the more prominent. Empirical research studies conducted in 1960s envisaged quality in education in two terms: School Effectiveness, and Accountability. Effectiveness is explained in terms of school assessment (Coleman and others). According to them school effectiveness is to be measured in quantitative terms. According to second view, education to child means all round development of a child. All round development means a child needs to be competent both in scholastic and non-scholastic achievements. Non-scholastic achievements are difficult to measure in quantitative terms, as these contain intangible elements. Therefore, quality in schools should be accountable to its targets. The schools, which achieve targets in time, are quality schools. According to this view, if curriculum and instructional process is weak and conventional, a school is not able to achieve the targets. It means if examination results are excellent, then the school offers quality in education (Winch, 1966).

At the end of twentieth century, another concept propped up, i.e., School Based Management (SBM). Holt (2000), while emphasising the importance of School Based Management, mentioned that SBM indicates the quality in education. In this process, the school gets freedom to design its own curriculum, offer a wide range of learning and assessment opportunities, with freedom and opportunities to innovate, enhance pupil engagement and thus offer quality.

In this context, a Board of Education has an important role to play, that is, regarding improving the quality in education; improving knowledge and skills of students; and improving standards of performance of students so that those who pass out would have necessary competence to handle things on their own.

Since the State Boards are principal agents in the secondary education to evaluate the educational objectives, no specific study yet has been done in the area of management of change and management of quality with respect to the role and involvement of the Boards.

Broadly, the quality of education at secondary and senior secondary stages depends upon three variables, i.e., curriculum planning, instructional mechanism in the schools, and evaluation and assessment.

Curriculum Planning and Development

India is a vast country with rich cultural heritage and wide dissimilarities in many aspects of social life. There is expansive diversity in geographical features, climate, culture, language and literature. Even economic conditions are not even. Therefore, it is not desirable to have a similar or identical curriculum and as such various committees and commissions from time to time have recommended to relate education to the needs and aspirations of the people in order to strengthen regional variations and to make it a forceful instrument of social, moral and other values, at the same time, according due recognition to the national integration. They emphasised that education and curricula to be effective must be in tune with cultural diversity, the emerging issues *vis-à-vis* the needs of children. The research experience over the last forty years concludes that though the technical skills remain the same all over the world, many educational objectives are not the same from school to school and from country to country. For example, skills taught in mathematics at secondary level may be same in India as well as in other countries, although the colonial history, culture and government of other countries are entirely different. Similarly, agricultural engineering basics taught in India could be similar to those taught in many other countries, but agricultural cropping has to relate the specific climatic and soil conditions of that country or for that matter with that region or area. Therefore, it is very essential that all the education Boards should address the issue whether students in a particular state are able to master skills being taught; so is the case with students in the neighbouring states. The Board authorities also need to recognise that there are common problems the world over, particularly management problems concerning 'inputs' to school quality. Reading material and reference books need to be provided for each subject, and curriculum from time to time needs to be reviewed and updated. The development and curriculum innovation have been the pursuit of the Boards over the years to make curriculum more relevant, meaningful, and life oriented.

In fact, at the national level, efforts to establish uniformity of standard has been stressed upon by NCERT in its documents, "The Curriculum for the Ten Year School – A Framework" published in 1975, and "Higher Secondary Education and Its Vocationalisation" in 1976. Again, in response to the recommendations of the NPE 1986, the NCERT also published "The National Curriculum for Elementary and Secondary Education—A Framework" in 1988. Another recent NCERT publication is the "National Curriculum Framework for School Education" (November 2000). It is up to the States now to adopt the NCERT suggestions with recommendation according to their own priorities.

Instructional Mechanism

At the national level, NCERT, and at the state level, State Council of Educational Research and Training (SCERTs), lead the country in designing exemplary instructional material on teacher education and providing training through innovative programmes. Because teachers are incharge of the teaching-learning process, they are expected to ensure that courses are completed on time. The external examiner judges the competence of teachers and the school. However, the external examination is conducted by the Board of School Education.

Evaluation and Assessment

Evaluation and assessment in the form of external examination is done by the Board of School Education. Evaluation is a process of collecting, analysing and interpreting evidences of students' achievement both in cognitive and non-cognitive areas of learning for purposes of taking a variety of decisions pertaining to certification, promotion and placement. Apart from these, evaluation has additional functions that include control of the curriculum and its delivery in the school, motivation of school, teachers and students, monitoring of educational standards and reporting of school effectiveness. Also an examination gives feedback to the school and teachers. Exam related data reveal strengths and weaknesses of the school. For example, a mathematics teacher may wish to find, 'why did more of students fail in mathematics this year than in the last year?' The head of a science department may like to investigate why students got higher grades in chemistry than in physics. Exam data also give detailed information on how candidates performed in each subject. This helps a school to identify weakness in its delivery of the curriculum and to rectify in future.

The backdrop suggests that Boards of Secondary Education are principal instrument for quality control. They direct the entire secondary education system in the country. Their primary aim is to manage change and quality in the education system that ultimately leads to change and quality in schools. Therefore, the present study has been taken up to understand how Boards are managing quality at the secondary level. The main objectives of the study are:

- To study procedures and roles performed by school Boards;
- To analyse activities undertaken by the Boards to improve quality of school education; and
- To suggest policy measures for better functioning of the Boards.

Methodology

The present research studied mainly the role played by the Boards in addition to being an examining body and to perceive the futuristic role to be played by them. In this study, observation and survey method was adopted, which enabled researcher to obtain information on various functions of the Boards as to how from time to time changes occurred in the policies and practices of the Boards with regard to improvement and quality of school education. An attempt is made to find out the present position of the Boards through description, recording, analysing and interpreting existing conditions. To know the perception of the Board officials, structured questionnaire and interview schedule were carried out mainly to gather information on the role in improving the quality of secondary education and accordingly to cope with management of change to maintain the quality of education.

Sampling

At present, there are 42 Secondary and Senior Secondary Boards. Some States have two or more Boards. The COBSE has the directory of all the Boards, in which all the Boards are listed zone-wise. Therefore, basis for selection of the Boards was COBSE directory. From four zones, i.e., North, South, East and West; one state was selected through stratified random sampling. From each state secondary and senior secondary Boards were selected. Andhra Pradesh state has two separate secondary and senior secondary Boards, but because of some administrative problems only secondary Board was selected for the study.

On the other hand, West Bengal state has three separate autonomous Education Boards: for Primary, Secondary and Higher Secondary Education. The focus of the study is only on secondary and senior secondary stages. Therefore Primary Education Board has been excluded from this study. Apart from these Boards, there are two other Boards, namely West Bengal Board of Madrasah Education, and Rabindra Mukta Vidyalaya. These two Boards also enjoy autonomous status. The examinations conducted by these Boards are equivalent to Secondary and Senior Secondary Examinations. Thus from east zone, i.e., West Bengal state, four Boards were included in the study. In all seven Boards were taken into consideration in this study.

- North Himachal Pradesh Board of School Education;
- West Board of Secondary Education, Madhya Pradesh;
- South Board of Secondary Education, Andhra Pradesh; and
- East West Bengal Board Secondary Education, West Bengal; Council of Higher Secondary Education; West Bengal Board of Madrasah Education; and Rabindra Mukta Vidyalaya

Data Collection

First of all, researcher consulted literature on Boards of Secondary Education, not only established in India but also of other countries, to know functioning of schools, structure of school education as well as functioning of Boards, to have a comparative approach. The data on 14 countries were collected to have an idea of the structure of education systems, policies, and types of secondary education and assessment procedures. The 14 countries are: the United States of America, England and Wales, France, Germany, Sweden, Ethiopia, Lesotho, Swaziland, Zambia, China, South Korea, Thailand and Japan.

The data was collected from primary as well as secondary sources. Primary sources contained two types of schedules: Interview Schedule and General Information Schedule. Interview Schedule was conducted on Chairman/President/Director of School Education Board. It was divided into five sections: general information, curriculum development, instructional material, evaluation strategy and capacity building. The schedule was used to gain information about the administration, functions of the Board and changes in policies that have been brought from time to time for the improvement of quality of education in general and improvement of school education in particular.

General Information Schedule tried to know the information on various aspects of Board, i.e., establishment of the Board, constitution of Board, strength of staff, size of the Board, number of students appeared and passed, professionals involved in paper-setting, about the training of teachers, details of income and expenditure of the Board, etc.

All the above information was collected by visiting the selected Boards of four States, i.e., Board of Secondary Education, Andhra Pradesh; Himachal Pradesh Board of School Education, Dharamshala; Board of Secondary Education, Madhya Pradesh; West Bengal Board of Secondary Education; West Bengal Council for Higher Secondary Education, West Bengal Board of Madrasah Education and Rabindra Mukta Vidyalaya. The researcher interviewed Chairmen/Presidents/ Directors of the Boards; Secretaries, Academic Registrars, Deputy Secretaries, Controllers of Examination, Budget and Accounts Officers, Academic Officers, Journal Editor, Chief System Officers, Deputy Directors, and Personal Relation Officers. The researcher also visited NCERT, COBSE offices. Apart from it, information was collected from Acts, Annual Reports of the Boards, Journals of

Boards, Education Code, Periodicals, Government Publications, Education Bulletins, Newspapers, etc.

Data Analysis

All information gathered from various sources was thoroughly looked into and analysed. Special emphasis was laid on the information of curriculum development, instructional mechanism, and evaluation and assessment procedures of the Boards. The opinion and views expressed by the Chairmen/Presidents/Directors of Boards of Education, and Secretaries of the Boards were summarised. The examination results and financial data were analysed. The statistical technique used for analysis was mainly in percentage or per cent increase or decrease from the base year.

2

Perspective on Secondary School System

Introduction

An attempt is made to look at the secondary education system across the countries (developed as well as developing) to have an idea of how changes have been made from time to time in the structure of education system, policies, types of secondary education and assessment procedures. The data on secondary education systems have been collected from 14 countries, i.e., United States of America, England and Wales, France, Germany, Sweden, Iceland, Ethiopia, Lesotho, Swaziland, Zambia, China, South Korea, Thailand and Japan.

United States of America

In the United States of America, the age of entry to compulsory education varies from state to state, it generally being 5 to 7 years, 6 being the most common age. The age of exiting varies between 16 and 18 years the most common being year 16. Secondary education in the US occurs in grades 7-12, depending upon the laws and policies of the concerned states and local school districts. There is no national structure, curriculum or governing law. All laws and policies are set and enforced by the state governments and local school districts. After 12th grade, certificate of the High School Diploma is awarded. This Diploma covers a variety of awards for different curricula and standards. There are honours/regents, academic/college preparatory, vocational and general/basic high school diploma tracks. There are minimum course requirements and other graduation requirements in each State, which usually correspond to the general/basic track.

Vocational and academic/college preparatory or honours/regents diplomas usually have additional set curricular requirements and standards which aspiring graduates must meet or exceed. In addition, majority of US secondary school districts and private schools permit students to participate in the Advanced Placement (AP) programme of the College Board. This programme allows qualified students to take college level introductory courses in selected subjects taught by a certified faculty.

The curriculum is reformed from time to time. Subjects generally recommended by leading educators are: classical modern languages; mathematics courses concerning algebra, geometry and trigonometry; science courses humanities – history, geography. Curriculum was earlier based on college entrance. During 1995, the Department of Education advocated that secondary school curriculum should be strengthened and enriched to include facets of life beyond the classroom. The early American education had stressed rote-learning and discipline. Schools in the twenty-first century stress rigorous studies that show students' correlation between studies and the occupations and endeavours they may undertake after graduation. Teachers involve students in an active way to acquire knowledge, rather than merely passively receive lectures.

The school follows the curriculum laid down by the particular state. Generally, teachers find innovative ways to teach that fully engage students in community service, work situations, thereby enabling the students to perceive the value of what they learn.

State authorities earlier used to be involved in the process of selecting and adopting textbooks. But later, teachers resisted such a procedure of selection of the textbooks offered by the committees appointed by the state department of education. For example, the National Council of Teachers of English, in May 1990, advanced a number of objections to state adopted textbooks that tended to control the curriculum and to limited professional choices of the teachers entrusted with the responsibility of teaching the material in the classroom. Teachers wanted to use the textbooks that they professionally felt most suitable. In many cases now, the academic freedom is given to teachers to change the text they believe will best prepare their students to understand course objectives.

Although elementary and secondary educators continue to put classroom emphasis on textbooks, but there is an upsurge in the use of Internet in schools since 1993. Many schools maintain a website;

nearly 9,000 elementary and secondary schools had websites up to 2001.

In USA, the system varies across states. Semester system based on credits is in vogue in schools and colleges. Five point grading system is in use. The following absolute grading scale is used in most schools and colleges.

Grade	*Range of Marks*
A	90-100
B	80-89
C	70-79
D	50-69
F	0-49

Grade F stands for fail in the semester. In addition to this, additional abbreviations included on the transcript are:

I	Incomplete
N	No credit
P	Credit for academic classes
K	Credit for non-academic classes
WP	Withdrawn after pass
WF	Withdrawn after fail

Examinations are offered in each AP subject at the end of an academic year. A score of 3 or higher generally results in universities awarding advanced standing in that subject, exempting the student from distribution requirements. A growing number of secondary schools also offer the International Baccalaureate (IB) as an optional track. Completion of IB usually requires an additional semester of study beyond the 12th year. The title 'High School Diploma' remains the most commonly recognised secondary school leaving certification. Contents of the curriculum leading to the diploma and grade obtained, are contained in the record of studies obtained, called *"High or Secondary School Transcript"*.

In Unites States examination system is not centralised. The job is left to private organisations, such as the Educational Testing Service, and the College Entrance Examination Board. Although these organisations do provide certain coherence to an educational system, but the equity aspect is hardly taken care of by these private organisations.

United Sates and Japan are the two countries that have rejected the traditional approach of examination, i.e., answer type of questions, because of cost and complexity of organising examinations. They have embraced the device of machine-scorable examinations, usually in the form of 'multiple-choice items'. This has been done largely because the commitment to widening the clientele served by examinations has been very strong and the numbers of candidates very large. A vast bank of items has been created through which actual question papers can be constructed. Development of written language skills among students is not a high priority. Their main aim is to develop tactics of guessing, recall type learning, rather than analysis and problem solving. Therefore, up to school level, students don't face challenge and when they enter colleges the first time, they face major demands upon their time and intellect.

Japan

The structure of education in Japan is 6-2-3. Compulsory education is of eight years, consisting of six-year primary course and two-year higher course, which is followed by three years of high school. For those students who complete the second year of the higher course and wish to continue their education, a special training course of one additional year is offered.

Curriculum Council is responsible for bringing reform in the education system. Serious efforts are made to analyse and respond to problems concerning curriculum in Japanese schools. Reforms suggested from time to time include: school system should emphasise on problem solving activities; independent thinking and use of computers in all subjects at all levels; and interdisciplinary courses that integrate content from diverse areas. Considerable emphasis is laid upon non-academic activities at middle level. Even then a curious phenomenon is seen among both the primary and the middle school children that is called 'school allergy'. The numbers of affected children have been rising sharply in recent decades because of fear of entrance exams.

In Japan, examination system is centralised. Entrance into higher education is on the basis of single, nation-wide, standardised examination. Just like the United States, they have adopted exclusive multiple-choice machine-scorable format for the university entrance examination. It is very economical as quantity of resources spent on it is quite low. In addition it provides higher levels of comparability across candidates and is generally more efficient to administer by examiners who are facing ever more and more number of candidates. Admission to university is based on the result of a test and competition for acceptance into the best schools is incredibly fierce.

Therefore, in order to improve control over the make-up of the entry classes, the colleges and universities have instituted a second level of examinations, set by each institution, thus effectively transforming the National Examination into a preliminary qualifying examination. This device has enabled the institutions of higher education in Japan to retain some measure of control over their recruitment, however at the cost of students and their parents. A large share of resource costs is borne by them, as they invest time and money in coaching after schools, and the expenses of travelling to distant cities to take the second-level examinations.

Therefore, growth of private coaching centres is mushrooming in Japan. These schools have turned into a huge business in Japan. The public has accepted it as a second school system that complements the public system and fills the space between what the conventional school teaches and what the next level of schooling and related exam require. It can be said that popularity of these coaching centres reflects the absolute failure of the Japanese educational system to prepare students for an academically rigorous future. The competition is putting psychological pressure on candidates. Indeed the competition is so intense and the pressures are so great during the secondary school period that the universities complain that students arrive burned-out, determined to make up for their lost youth, and unwilling to continue to study hard. This phenomenon worries many Japanese leaders and it has led to a re-evaluation of the average number of hours students spend in school each year.

Japan continues to emphasise the use of technology in education at all levels. A Study by Makasore (1999) mentioned that computers were used in 97.9 per cent of primary schools, 95.9 per cent of lower secondary schools and 100 per cent of upper secondary schools. Moreover, audio-visual media are widely used in Japan, especially in primary schools. Television audiotapes and videotapes are common gadgets for teaching. In 1999, Ministry of Education started a television station devoted exclusively to the education of Japan's children—'Children Broadcasting Station'. The channels beam programmes by communication satellite to receiving stations that have telephone links. When the station broadcasts programmes on the second and fourth Saturdays of each month (school holidays), children are encouraged to send faxes back to the television guest and take part in videoconferences.

England and Wales

Compulsory education is from 5-16 years age. About 90 per cent of the state secondary school students in England and Wales go to comprehensive schools, which provide a wide range of secondary education for children of all abilities. Policy and overall funding for education is determined by the Department of Education. The curriculum is nationalised. The curriculum sets out what pupils should study, what they should be taught and the standards that they should achieve. During the General Certificate of Secondary Education (GCSE), examination system was started in place of the dual system of CSE and GCE O-level.

The GCSE is of two types – A level, and A2 level, with regular in-school based assessments. The A-level is based entirely on a modular approach in which candidates can take modules as they proceed through the course, rather than only being examined in a single session at the end of the course. All students take the Advanced Subsidiary (AS) and then, where appropriate, proceed to the more challenging A2 after completion of their A level. The second year of the full A-level is called A2. A2 modules do not make up a qualification in their own right. Course work contributes to the result. There is a course work limit with a ceiling of 30 per cent in most subjects for A-level. They are graded from A-E. New Advanced Extension Awards (AEAs) have been developed which are designed to stretch the most able; these have been based on revised special papers (S levels), made available for first examination in summer 2002. Vocationally oriented qualifications are available in the form of National Vocational Qualification (NVQs), General National Vocational Qualifications (GNVQs) and Vocational A levels.

Iceland

The structure of education in Iceland is ten years basic education and four years upper secondary education. The education is compulsory up to basic education. The upper secondary education is governed by law enacted in 1996. Ministry issues National Curriculum Guidelines describing the content and objectives of each programme of study. There are four types of upper secondary schools:

1. General academic schools that offer four-year academic programmes concluding with matriculation examination that is required for entrance into the higher education programmes.
2. Industrial vocational schools offering theoretical and practical programme of study in skilled and some non-skilled trades.
3. Comprehensive schools that provide programmes of study comparable to those offered in the general academic and vocational industrial schools in addition to other specialised vocational training programmes.
4. Vocational schools that offer programmes of study designed for specialised employment.

Students in vocational programmes are given the opportunity to complete additional course work if they are interested in university studies or they can follow vocational training in such fields as Agriculture, Fishing, Industry, Food Production, or Health or Commerce.

General academic education is organised into three subjects that all students are required to enroll for specialised subjects that fit with the aims of particular programmes and electives. There are three different academic programmes leading to matriculation (foreign languages, natural sciences and social sciences). A shorter academic programme is designed for students who are undecided about what particular course of study to pursue and for those who need additional preparation prior to committing to the longer academic track or vocational programme.

The National Curriculum Guidelines prescribe the framework for individual courses of study, including the content, duration and assessment requirements. At the end of each semester, examinations are held and grades on other course assignments are figured into the final grades. For the skilled trades, there are journeyman's and nationally coordinated subject area exams. Upper-secondary schools are required by law to write School Working Guides describing programme offerings, teaching methods employed, and the role of the administration. They must also regularly conduct sequenced self-evaluations addressing teaching, administration and communication.

France

The structure of education system in France is 5-4-3. France operates a centralised education system. Ministry of National Education is responsible for the whole initial education system and has alternative tracks in the education system. It lays down not only the content of the different Baccalaureate series, but also the nature and content of all the different short-cycle vocational courses, in which vocationally related education is more fully integrated with core academic schooling, and both syllabus and assessment are coordinated and administered centrally by government officials. All technical diplomas involve consultation with the Occupational Consultative Committee. After discussion, decision about setting up or discontinuing diplomas are taken.

In France, secondary schools are divided into: *Sixieme* for 1 year; *Cinquieme* and *Quatrieme* for 2 years; and the final *Troisieme* for 1 year. *Sixieme* means final year of elementary school. The secondary education is divided into two successive stages, i.e., from 11-15 years and 16 to 18 years. Almost all children attend first stage. Since 1975 there has been a single mixed ability school for all students regardless of their level of achievement. After that they move onto a general, technical or vocational *lycee.* These prepare students for the corresponding Baccalaureate examinations, which is normally at the age of 18. The changes made in the Baccalaureate represent bold and on the whole successful moves. Vocational education takes place entirely within the basic system of schooling.

After completing compulsory education some students enter short-cycle technical education, which takes place in the vocational schools (*lycees*). A very few go into longer cycle options which can themselves be either technical or general.

First national examination, Baccalaureate, is held at the *Troisieme* and diploma is awarded on the basis of each student's course grades achieved in all classes taken during *Quatrieme* and *Troisieme* (these grades are counted with a coefficient of 1), as well as in combination with a timed written examination in French, Mathematics and History-Geography (with a coefficient of 2). The pupil who wants to go to higher secondary education has to attain a score of 10 out of 20. The success rate of secondary education is 75 per cent.

Thus three main and quite different options are open to students of diploma holders at higher secondary level: the General Baccalaureate (three years) leads to the university and to specialised schools of higher education (highly competitive entrance examination); Second Technological Baccalaureate (three years) that opens to various specialised schools of technological, professional or artistic sort; and Third Professional Baccalaureate (two years), that leads directly to induction into the job market. The course curriculum is quite complex and recognises many goals and levels. Every student makes his own decision concerning his or her eventual path and teachers and parents are closely involved in this process.

Germany

The German education system provides different paths for students based on individual ability. Children enter at age 6, and students of all levels of ability remain together as a group through the fourth grade, when most students are around 10 years old. The German school system tracks students of differing abilities and interests into different school forms. In spite of the far-reaching changes of the past 30 years, including the shift from elite to mass education, Germany's traditional three-tiered system of education at the secondary level remains intact. In addition, support for this system remains strong among teachers, students, and parents of differing educational and social class backgrounds.

At the primary stage, teachers recommend their students to a particular school, based on criteria such as academic achievement, potential, personality characteristics, like ability to work independently and self-confidence. However, in most states parents have the final say as to which school their child will track to following the fourth grade, and some parents go against the teacher's recommendation because they believe the higher level tracks offer their children more opportunities.

In most states, there are three types of schools at the lower secondary level:

1. Schools that have grades 5-9, which lead to receipt of certificate and then to part-time enrollment in a vocational school combined with apprenticeship training until the age of 18.
2. Schools that have grades 5-10 which lead to receipt of certificate and then to part-time vocational schools, higher vocational schools or continuation of study at a *Gymnasium.*
3. Schools that have grades 5-13, which prepare students for university study or for a dual academic and vocational credential.

The *Berufsschule* is an upper secondary school form which students may enter following the successful completion of either the 5-9 grade 9 *(Hauptschule)* or 5-10 grade *(Realschule)* to pursue part-time academic study combined with apprenticeship. The successful completion of an apprenticeship programme leads to certification in a particular trade or field of work. Unlike the general education, which is under the direct control of local and regional authorities, the responsibility for Germany's dual system, which combines education with vocational apprenticeships, is shared by the Government, a national coordinating and advisory body, the federal government, the states, representatives from industry, commerce, the trades and trade unions, and vocational teachers. School is compulsory between the ages of six and 15. Education is primarily a responsibility of the states, and the educational system varies from state to state.

Students from the schools that have grades 5-13, after completion of secondary education, enter into vocational training, a combination of work-based training and attendance of a part-time vocational school. Training normally takes three or three and a half years. There are only a few occupations (such as sales assistant) where training is of less than three years. Students have to first acquire basic vocational skills and knowledge, special training begins after that.

Assessment is done through grading. The grading scale runs from one (the best mark) to six (five in Austria). Students receiving a poor mark of five or six in several subjects may have to repeat a year, but this is rare.

Sweden

The Swedish state school system comprises compulsory schooling up to the age of 16 years (lower secondary stage). In 1971, Sweden introduced a new form of upper secondary schooling, designed to continue the education of a very large fraction of the post-compulsory age-group, and to integrate three formerly separate types of schools (*gymnasium*, vocational school and continuation school). There are twenty-seven programmes of two or three years' duration. Some of these programmes are highly academic (especially the natural sciences stream); others are more vocationally oriented; yet others are 'general'. Post-secondary studies include advanced vocational training which is intended to meet the labour market's needs with the skills required for modern production of goods and services. About one-third of the course period takes place at the workplace. As from

January 2002, this form of training is a permanent part of the Swedish educational system but does not belong to the higher education sector. Admission is based on three-year upper secondary education or corresponding proficiency. The training is intended to correspond to at least two years of study and to lead to a Certificate of Advanced Vocational Training.

In the mid-1970s, Sweden discarded the final secondary school examination system in order to reduce the strain on pupils. In place of the final examination, the Swedes installed a combination of marks gained during regular classroom and homework and in nationally set tests administered at intervals during the school career. Meanwhile, in 1977, a major reform of the higher education system revamped admission criteria. Work experience and age were given strong weightage in the admission decision, and completing a less demanding upper secondary school line was not by itself considered sufficient for admission to higher education. Additional study and credential were demanded.

Abandonment of final examinations was also motivated by the desire to improve the diagnostic and predictive value of tests of individual student's achievement and to give teachers national benchmarks against which to set their own pedagogical efforts. The Swedes have been willing to incur rather heavy costs to achieve these goals. The new system requires time-consuming collaboration among teachers in a given school, and across schools in a region. Exceptionally detailed record keeping is required, and the Swedish National Board of Education is charged with the responsibility of preparing and standardising the tests given in the basic school subjects at various points along the school ladder. Although Sweden may have abandoned its final secondary school examination, there has been no abandonment of tests and examinations in general. Indeed, one might well argue that there is now more examining and evaluation based on tests and examinations than ever before. External examinations have thus been replaced by continuous assessment, nationally planned but locally executed. Regular evaluation of the entire Swedish school system is supposed to provide the data on which any necessary remedial actions can be based.

Ethiopia

In Ethiopia, education structure is 8-2-2, i.e., eight years of primary education, two years of lower secondary education, and two years of extended polytechnic education. From the polytechnic education streams the students go to academic science or arts (upper secondary) or to two years of extended technical and vocational education (extended presently to three years).

Lesotho

In Lesotho, education structure is 7-3-2: seven years of primary school, which leads to the Primary School Leaving Examination; a junior secondary school offering three years of secondary schooling, leading to the Junior Certificate Examination. This is followed by a two-year course in a senior secondary school, leading to the Cambridge Overseas School Certificate. Various home economics and craft schools offer courses for primary school leavers. Two trade schools offer two or three-year diploma and certificate courses for holders of the Junior Certificate.

Swaziland

The education system of Swaziland consists of primary, secondary and post secondary education. The age of entry into primary school is 6 years and the cycle or duration is seven years, which means students theoretically finish primary education when they are 12 years old.

Secondary education is divided into two sub-levels. The junior level has a duration of three years, while the senior level is of two years duration. Students who pass the junior level obtain a Junior Certificate and proceed to take the Cambridge O-Level examination, which offers a General Certificate of Education (GCE) for entry to tertiary institutions and to university. Of the Government budget, approximately 25 per cent is spent on education. Of this, 35 per cent is spent on primary, 29 per cent on secondary and 22 per cent on higher education. Although universal primary education has been achieved, there are still insufficient schools and classrooms to meet the demand for secondary education.

Zambia

In Zambia, primary education is of seven years duration. The secondary school system is divided into two parts: Junior Secondary consisting of Grades 8 and 9, and Senior Secondary consisting of Grades 10-12.

The above four African countries, i.e., Ethiopia, Lesotho, Swaziland and Zambia, possess educational systems, which are markedly pyramidal—broad at the bottom and narrowing right from the second grade onwards. The system of examination in all these countries was heavily influenced by traditional British examination procedures and some American's way. The examinations are formal, terminal, subject-based and externally administered by either the Ministry of Education or Examination Council closely related to the Ministry. In the examination, the emphasis was on written work rather than on the assessment of practical, oral or course work. But Africa has not escaped from the wind of change in assessment. The changes that have been incorporated are: essay-type written examinations have been replaced in part or in whole by multiple-choice tests, and also continuous assessment has been introduced in parallel with the external examination at secondary level. External examinations exist in all the four African countries at the end of primary schooling, at the end of the junior cycle of secondary schooling and at the end of senior cycle of secondary schooling. Examinations play a critical role in taking admission to next grade as well as they are also used for certification as employers take account of students' educational achievements as indicated by the certificates they have obtained. Now-a-days examinations in these countries have also been started to relate with accountability. Schools with good examination results are regarded as good schools. Attempts to provide more adequate sampling curricula in examinations suggest, in addition to a concern for curricular validity, a concern for the education of children rather than for just the ones that are likely to be selected to continue in the educational system. A detailed feedback on examination performance is provided to schools rather than just grades of students.

There is a state control on examination system. However, the control varies somewhat from country to country. In some countries, the Ministry of Education administers the system and in others Examination Councils look after this function. Looking at the interest of the country, teachers are involved in syllabus committees, in setting of papers, in supervision and in examining and other forms of assessment.

Russian Federation

Schooling is centralised and uniform in the Russian Federation. The structure of education system in Russian Federation is 4-5-2. The primary and secondary levels, usually combined in one school, represent general education. The primary education is of 3 or 4 years, basic secondary of 5 years, and upper secondary is of 2 years. The secondary school system is of two types. After basic secondary course, students can either go on to the upper level or enter one of the secondary professional schools.

In early 1990's schools acquired the right to choose curricula and textbooks, to diversify the teaching process and introduce different profiles of education. In schools, Parent-Teacher Associations' are formed; they assist the teachers and the administrations.

From 1992 onwards, a new approach has been introduced for structuring of the permanent and variable parts of the curricula. They include federal, national and regional components. Federal component defines the obligatory minimum content of educational programmes, maximum workload and the required level of student training. In their turn, the national and regional components reflect the specific needs of a particular locality and ethnic group. The standards have to be reviewed at least in ten years.

The democratisation of the school system, greater flexibility in curricula development, and encouragement of innovations have opened up the way to numerous experiments at the secondary level. In 1998-99, alongside the regular secondary schools, innovative secondary schools and non-traditional humanitarian schools were opened. In innovative secondary schools, the need for specialisation in particular areas (mathematics, law, ecology and pedagogy) was stressed upon. In the second type, study of at least two foreign languages is essential.

Apart from this, Russia has schools for gifted and talented children. These schools which work in conjunction with theatres and conservations, provide advanced training in ballet, music and performing arts. Children with outstanding abilities for mathematics, biology, physics and other sciences, selected during nationwide competitions (Olympiads), are enrolled in specialised educational establishments, which are affiliated to universities and serve as laboratory schools or experimental grades. Those who decide to combine work with secondary education can study at part-time evening schools.

In schools, specialised professional education is strongly encouraged. Many types of schools are in existence, like Artillery School, Medical School, Engineering School, Navy Academy and other such institutions.

Vocational institutions were established to meet the needs of particular territories. New types of schools combined general and vocational training with the purpose to improve the students' economic, legal and industrial competence. The system encompasses two levels of education: professional technical schools, and centres of continuing professional education, which train skilled workers and para-professionals for blue-collar jobs. Types of schools at the secondary professional level include polytechnics that specialise for non-production jobs, like pre-primary and primary school teachers, nurses, circus performers, and librarians. Other types of vocational institutions are farmers' schools, commercial schools and specialised schools aimed at the social rehabilitation of juvenile delinquents.

To attract the students for vocational training, educators try to diversify curricula, financial reform of the network, and cooperation of the state, businesses, trade unions and educational intuitions. The educational process consists of lectures, tutorials, laboratory work, consultations, tests, excursions, simulation games and practical training. The weekly study load is 36 to 38 hours. Vocational schools are administered by a council representing all categories of employees, students and other interested parties (enterprises, organisations, or parents).

All the secondary schools students receive a cumulative grade in each subject at the end of the academic year. Officially the grading is based on a four point scale: 5, excellent; 4, good; 3, fair; and 2, poor (failure). Grade 1 (very poor) is usually an emotional response to unsatisfactory performance and is used as a disciplinary measure. Students with a failing grade in one subject are allowed to go to the next grade, but they have to complete their work and the particular subject. Students who are unable to cope with a particular level cannot go on to the next level.

Excellent students of grades five to eight are exempt from examinations. But everybody is required to take exams after grade nine, as it is final year and basic secondary school.

Director is responsible for general management of the school and heads the school. He/she looks after educational process, staffing, the financial state of the school, the maintenance of its facilities, as well as food and security. Deputy Directors take care of particular areas of work, like curricula, schedules, extracurricular activities etc. In school, pedagogical council is chaired by the Director who is responsible for governing the school. The council includes all Deputy

Directors and staff. Decisions about each and every aspect of school functioning is taken by this committee, like organisational structure of school administration, educational programmes, choice of curricula, forms and methods of teaching, approving the students' final grades, cooperation with the parents' committee, educational institutions, and NGOs.

South Korea

In South Korea, school education comprises six years of elementary schooling, three years of middle school and three years of high school. Since 1980, Korean government is trying to make secondary education compulsory, but has strongly controlled the expansion of higher education for fear of creating an oversupply of college graduates for available jobs. Tough competition exists for admission to higher education courses. Therefore, many educational problems arise as for Koreans education is regarded as a means for personal advancement. As such, traditionally admission to an advanced school is very important to most people. In order to solve these problems, many educational policies have been carried out so far. The equalisation policy for secondary schools is one of them. To correct the entrance exam problems, of the primary school, middle schools and high schools entrance examinations were abolished and a lottery system was introduced in the system.

The curriculum is centralised. MOE and the Korea Institute of Curriculum and Evaluation are responsible for developing the national curriculum at elementary, middle and high school levels. The national curriculum and regional guidelines allow schools to adopt textbooks according to their individual characteristics and objectives. National curriculum is subject to periodic revisions. Main objectives of sixth and seventh national curriculum are democratisation and local autonomy to allow flexibility to meet individual needs and to enhance character creativity and diversity, while imparting basic knowledge. In high schools, students have to study all subjects rather than concentrating on a few chosen subjects at a time as in the US. There is a unique option for students at college level. If a student has taken admission in a particular course including medical, he has the freedom of changing major and specific courses.

Three types of textbooks are used in the schools, i.e., published by MOE; published by private publishers and authorised by MOE;

and published by private publishers and recognised by MOE. Individual schools have the freedom to choose textbooks to meet the students' needs.

Contemporary Koreans are firm believers in use of technology. By 2001, every teacher had his/her own PC, and every elementary and secondary school in Korea was connected to a Local Area Network (LAN) and the Internet—the first such achievement in the world.

The MOE established a computer education development plan in 1988, which supported computer assisted instructions in schools and computerisation of school administrations.

To meet the demand of a high-tech industrial society, several measures have been adopted, which include recruiting bright students into science and technology via scholarships and other privileges. Faculty members are encouraged to conduct joint research, promote internship programmes and conduct seminars.

The Korea multi-media Education Centre and the Korea Research Information Centre have been developing high quality software and an electronic platform to support the research activities of teachers. They also operate the cyber schools for students' self-instruction to a certification system for excellence in commercial education software.

Thailand

In Thailand, education system is of 6-3-3 pattern. It is followed by a wide variety of post-secondary options. Secondary schools educate children between the ages of 12 to 17 and are overseen by Ministry of Education and local municipalities in the public sector and by the Private Education Commission in the private schools. Secondary schools are divided into lower and upper secondary. A comprehensive or diversified curriculum that combine general education with work experience has been introduced at lower secondary level. Further secondary education is divided into two basic tracks: general academic, and vocational. Of students in upper secondary, 57 per cent take general academic track and 43 per cent the vocational. The curriculum of both lower and upper secondary have four basic elements; core subjects, such as Thai language, Mathematics, Science, and English, which must be taken by all students; the elective subjects that differ according to local conditions and needs; free elective subjects, depending on the interests of the learners; and activities.

China

The structure of education system in China is of 5-3-3 pattern. Secondary education and training has two parts: the formal part and the informal part. Three years are for junior secondary that is uniform and compulsory and the remaining three years are for senior secondary schools which are divided into four parts: general senior secondary, technical or specialised secondary, vocational secondary, and craftsmen schools. By 1998, 45 per cent of senior secondary students were enrolled in the general education track, whereas the other 55 per cent were enrolled in the specialisation tracks.

General secondary education is managed by the Ministry of Education, and the vocational and technical secondary schools are directed by Technical Ministries as well as by the Ministry of Education. There are four levels of government: national, provincial, county and local level. The basic administrative unit is county. Two major reforms extended compulsory education to include lower secondary and diversified education at the senior high school level. Several transformations have been done in rural secondary education. In 1985, educational reform legislation officially placed rural secondary schools under local administration. In 1987, there were four kinds of secondary vocational and technical schools: technical schools that offered a four-year, post-junior middle course and two-to-three-year post-senior middle training in such fields as commerce, legal work, fine arts, and forestry; workers' training schools that accepted students whose senior-middle-school education consisted of two years of training in such trades as carpentry and welding; vocational technical schools that accepted either junior-or-senior-middle-school students for one to three-year courses in cooking, tailoring, photography, and other services; and agricultural middle schools that offered basic subjects and agricultural science. By 1990, China had come close to meeting its goal of vocationalising one-half of its senior secondary schools.

These technical schools had several hundred different programmes. Their narrow specialisation had advantages in that they offered in-depth training, reducing the need for on-the-job training and thereby lowering learning time and costs. Moreover, students were more motivated to study if there were links between training and future jobs. Much of the training could be done at existing enterprises, where staff and equipment were available at little additional cost. The Chinese education also relies heavily on local private donations and incomes generated by schools themselves. These non-government contributions amounted to 32.3 per cent of the total educational expenditure.

From 2000, an attempt was made in Beijing primary schools to place 100 marks system by a grading system describing performance in terms of four grades: Excellent, Good, Pass and Fail. Sixty per cent of each grading is based on overall achievement in a subject and remaining 40 per cent on daily behaviour of a student.

Conclusions

It is observed that in all the above countries whose educational systems were studied, educational reforms have been a hot topic of discussion in recent years. At all levels, from kindergarten to university, critics have been calling for changes in the traditional way of running schools. Although everyone agrees that there are problems in education, not everyone agrees on just what changes are needed. For the purposes of this study, the following conclusions can be drawn:

1. The structure of educational system across the countries is a three-tiered system (primary, secondary and higher education).
2. Education is compulsory either up to elementary level or up to secondary level. In Japan, Korea, Thailand, China, Ethiopia, Lesotho, Swaziland and Zambia, education is compulsory up to elementary level, while in others, mostly in the developed countries, education is compulsory up to secondary level. Age group for compulsory education is either up to 14 or 15, except in the United States of America, South Korea, France, England and Wales. In these countries, age for compulsory education is up to 16, i.e., up to secondary education.
3. Time spent in the primary stage ranges from four to eight years, with six years being the most common. Russia, Germany, England and Wales have the shortest primary stage system with four-year duration, and Iceland, Ethiopia, Lesotho, Swaziland and Zambia have the longest primary stage duration. Similarly, the age of entry to primary schools ranges from five years of age to seven years, with six being the most common. South Korea, England and Wales have the youngest entry age of five years. At the lower/junior secondary stage, the most common duration is three years

and the most common age of entry is twelve years. At the upper, higher or pre-university stage, the duration is split fairly to two and three years, and 15 years is the most common age of entry.

4. In most of the countries, secondary education is divided into stages, although the point of demarcation varies. In the United States of America, France, South Korea, and Iceland, there is a single stage and in China, Italy, Russia, Japan, Thailand, Ethiopia, Zambia, Swaziland and Lesotho, secondary schools have two stages.
5. Secondary education is divided into two lower and upper secondary stages. Further, these stages are divided according to the curriculum. In most of the countries, lower secondary stage emphasises on general education, which may or may not be designed to prepare students for more specialised study. However, Thailand has introduced comprehensive or diversified curriculum that combines general education with work experience at lower secondary level. In the same way, in Germany lower secondary level is divided into three tracks, i.e., technical education, academically oriented and vocational education. In Lesotho, various economics and crafts schools offer courses for primary school leavers. Two trade schools offer two-or three-year diploma and certificate courses for holders of the Junior Certificate.
6. In most cases, the classification of secondary education takes effect only at the upper secondary stage. Whenever such classification exists, it is mainly into two types: general/academic and vocational. Apart from aforementioned classification of schools, other types of secondary schools in America include comprehensive secondary or special secondary schools. In the Russian Federation, many types of schools are in existence, like Artillery School, Medical School, Engineering School, Navy Academy and other institutions. In Iceland, four types of upper secondary schools exist—general academic, industrial vocational, comprehensive, and vocational. In Germany special schools are offered for students with mental or physical disabilities. In China four types of senior secondary schools exist general, technical or specialised, vocational and crafts.
7. Student's inclination is moving towards vocational and

technical education, as there are links between training and future jobs. For instance in Thailand 57 per cent students opt for general education and 43 per cent opt for vocational education, while in China 45 per cent students opt for general education and 55 per cent for specialised education.

8. Educational technology is gaining importance across the countries. Japan continues to emphasise the use of technology in education at all levels. In Russia computer literacy is a part of curriculum at all levels of education and contemporary Koreans are firm believers of educational technology. The Korea Multi-media Education Centre and the Korea Research Information Centre have been developing high quality software and an electronic platform to support the research activities of teachers. They also operate the cyber schools for students' self-instruction to a certification system for excellence in commercial education software.
9. The common characteristics in the school education are that all its stages are linked with each other through examination mechanism. Examination has been described as the backbone of our educational system. It is generally administered at the end of the year. The United States of America, England and Wales, France, Germany and Sweden have replaced the formal examination with continual assessment at all grades and levels of secondary education, while Thailand, Japan, South Korea and African countries, i.e., Ethiopia, Lesotho, Swaziland and Zambia stress on continuous assessment in parallel with external examination for promotion of students for the next higher grade. But in Korea and Japan, admission to higher education is on the basis of performance in the final examination.
10. In Germany, grading scale runs from 1 (the best mark) to 6. Students receiving a poor mark of 6 in several subjects may have to repeat a year, but this is rare. In place of the final examination, the Swedes installed a combination of marks gained during regular classroom transactions and homework and in nationally set tests administered at intervals during the school career. Abandonment of final examinations was also motivated by the desire to improve the diagnostic and predictive value of tests of individual student achievement

and to give teachers national benchmarks against which to set their own pedagogical efforts. These include weekly/ monthly/term class tests, projects and regular class assignments set by respective teachers of the subject. In the selection and promotion of students to the next higher grade of secondary education, only the summative examination grades are considered. In France, secondary school certificate Baccalaureate is awarded on the basis of grades in all the classes taken during four years, i.e., 11-15 years.

11. Another noteworthy feature of examination scene is that US, Japan, Ethiopia, Lesotho, Swaziland and Zambia have started embracing the device of machine-scorable examinations, usually in the form of collections of 'Multiple Choice Items'.
12. US and Germany have much less federal educational control and uniformity in education is primarily a responsibility of the states or cantons, and the educational system may vary from state to state. In rest of the countries, education system has centralised control.
13. Curriculum is centralised in all the countries, except in the United States and Russian Federation. There is no national structure in US curriculum or governing law; all laws and policies are set and enforced by the state governments and local school districts. However, all the countries are moving towards the process of decentralisation. To enhance creativity and diversity, while imparting basic knowledge, emphasis is laid in Korea on local autonomy to meet individual needs. Japan has started emphasising in the curriculum on independent thinking, problem solving activities and use of computers in all the subjects and inter-disciplinary courses with stress on non-academic activities. In Germany, the curriculum focuses mostly on academic subjects, even in vocational schools, with a limited offering of physical education, sports, art, and music. Religious instruction is required, but students over the age of 14 can opt out. In Russian Federation, a new approach has been introduced for structuring of the permanent and variable parts of the curricula. They include federal, national and regional components. Federal component defines the obligatory minimum content of educational programmes,

maximum workload and the required level of student training. In their turn, the national and regional components reflect the specific needs of a particular locality and ethnic group. The standards have to be reviewed at least after ten years. In Thailand, a comprehensive or diversified curriculum that combines general education with work experience has been introduced at lower secondary level.

To conclude, the role of examination is to improve the quality of education. It determines what goes on in the classrooms in terms of 'what' and 'how' teachers teach and students learn and can have an impact on both teaching and learning. There is no best way to assess what students have learned and teachers have taught. May be one method works in one country and another method in other country. For improving the quality of education, it is imperative that the process of formative evaluation is strengthened, and implementation of continuous and comprehensive evaluation is sincerely followed.

3

Himachal Pradesh School Education Board

The structure of school education in Himachal Pradesh is ten years of secondary schooling and two years of senior secondary schooling, known as 10+2 system. Out of the 12 years of schooling, primary education consists of 5 years, upper primary education 3 years, secondary education 2 years, and senior secondary education 2 years (Table 3.1). In Himachal Pradesh, there are 1246 secondary schools and 708 senior secondary schools. The enrolment in these schools is 1.38 lakhs and 0.72 lakh at secondary and senior secondary levels respectively.

Table 3.1: Education Structure

Age	*Education Stage*	*Classes*
06-11	Primary	I-V
11-14	Upper Primary	VI-VIII
14-16	Secondary	IX-X
16-18	Senior Secondary	XI-XII

Table 3.2 gives the scenario of growth of secondary and senior secondary schools in the state. The secondary schools increased from 1168 to 1246 from 1996-97 to 2001-02. In the same way, senior secondary schools increased from 421 to 708 from 1996-97 to 2001-02. The percentage increase of number of senior secondary schools, (68.17) was quite substantial as compared to secondary schools (6.68). In secondary schools negative percentage increase observed during 1998-99 and 1999-2000 may be because a number of secondary schools were upgraded to senior secondary during the period.

The instructional days per year in HP schools are 180 instead of 200 because of difficult terrain, inclement weather and tough topography. However, the numbers of school hours per day are 6 hours as per national norms.

Table 3.2: Growth of Educational Institutes at Secondary and Senior Secondary Level

Year	*Growth of Educational Institutes*					
	Secondary	*% Increase*	*Senior Secondary*	*% Increase*	*Total*	*Total % Increase*
1996–97	1168	–	421	–	1589	–
1997–98	1169	00.09	462	9.74	1631	2.64
1998–99	1028	–11.99	497	18.05	1525	–4.02
1999–00	1040	–10.96	523	24.23	1563	–1.63
2000–01	1183	01.28	649	54.16	1632	2.70
2002–03	1246	06.68	708	68.17	1954	2.29

Source: *Selected Educational Statistics 1996-97 to 2002-03*, Department of Education, and Ministry of HRD.

HP Board of School Education

Prior to the establishment of HP Board of School Education, the Panjab University, Chandigarh, was performing the functions of conducting public examinations in respect of secondary and senior secondary schools and matters connected therewith. Over the years as number of students increased, the functions of the university also increased. Due to large number of students many complex problems arose. Therefore, demand for setting up Board of School Education in Himachal Pradesh was felt. It was in this context that the HP Board of School Education came into existence in 1969 through an Act No. 14 of 1968. Until 1982, the Board had it's headquarters at Shimla, which was subsequently shifted in 1983 to Dharamshala in Kangra District. The headquarters of HP Education Board, Dharamshala, is located at the foothills of the Dhauladhur ranges of western Himalayas overlooking picturesque Kangra valley of HP.

The Education Board prescribes syllabi, courses of instructions and textbooks for school education in HP besides conducting examinations based on such courses. At present, the Board conducts examinations for the VIII, X, XI and XII classes. In addition, the Board also conducts departmental examination for Junior Basic

Teachers Certificate (JBTC), Trained Teachers Certificate (TTC), Physical Education Training Certificate (PETC), and Diploma in Education. As many as over two lakhs candidates appear annually in the examinations conducted by the Board.

Role and Functions of the Board

The study concentrates primarily on three aspects: curriculum, instruction and evaluation. Therefore functions of the Board according to the Act are divided into these sub-heads.

Curriculum

- Prescribes syllabi and publishes textbooks for school education in HP.
- Arranges for the preparation, writing, compilation, printing, publishing and sale of textbooks, other educational material and undertakes the publication of any other educational work, books or periodicals.
- Adopts measures to promote the physical, moral, cultural and social welfare of students in recognised institutions and prescribes conditions of their residence and discipline.
- Organises and provides lectures, demonstrations and educational exhibitions, seminars and symposiums, and takes such other measures as necessary to raise and promote the quality of school education in HP.
- Takes necessary steps with regard to the modernising of school curricula, strengthening of science and mathematics education, work experience and vocationalisation.
- Organises research for grading of external vocabulary and arranges for regular revision of textbooks and other books.

Instruction

- Prescribes courses of instruction in schools.
- Prescribes standards that the schools and other institutions seeking affiliation with the Board ought to fulfill in terms of teachers and their qualifications, curriculum, equipment, buildings, and other educational facilities.

Examination

- Admits to its examination, on conditions that may be prescribed, to candidates who pursue the prescribed course of instructions, for recognised institutions and for private institutions.

- Publishes the results.
- Grants diplomas or certificates to persons who pass the examination of the Board.
- Institutes and awards scholarships, medals and prizes under conditions that may be prescribed.
- Conducts the departmental examination.
- Appoints paper-setters, translators, the examiners, moderators and supervisory staff, and fixes their remuneration for conducting the final examinations for evaluation of candidate's performance and for compiling and releasing of results.
- Opens centres for the final examinations conducted by it.
- Declares the results of candidates at the final examinations conducted by it.
- Lays down procedures to deal with cases of use of unfair means in the examinations and deals with such cases.
- Generally evaluates the performance of students in all examinations in secondary and senior secondary schools including the final examinations and makes from time to time, necessary recommendations in respect of the same to the government.
- Institutes and awards scholarships, medals and prizes under conditions that may be prescribed.

Thrust Areas of the Board

On the basis of the above functions, the thrust areas of the Board are as follows:

I. Instruction (Teaching-Learning Process)

Teaching-learning process takes place in the school on the basis of textbooks prescribed by the Board. HP Board approves syllabi through its subject committees, based on the directions given by the NCERT.

The textbooks are written by experienced teachers, which are approved by the Board's textbook committee. When the Board was established, the textbooks were printed by leading printers and printing paper was supplied by the Government of India to printers on subsidized rates. But later the Board modified its policy with regard to school textbooks. The Board took the responsibility of publication and printing of textbooks, and distribution of textbooks was carried out through private booksellers apart from depots of the Boards and book co-operatives. The change in policy was made so that the students should get textbooks in time. There is a provision of free textbooks up to PG level for girls and for SC/ST/OBC up to higher secondary levels.

II. Curriculum

For all matters concerning curriculum, Academic Committee of the Board takes the decisions. The Academic Committee has the power to prescribe syllabus as well as make changes in the curriculum.

- During 1983-84, syllabi for Classes I to X were prepared, and the Sanskrit portion in Hindi subject for middle classes was simplified. The syllabi of the subjects of Tamil and Telgu for the Classes IX and X were prepared. These languages have been introduced as third language.
- In 2001-02, the Board got reviewed Class X Mathematics syllabus by an experts committee.
- Physical education and information technology subjects were included in the curriculum in 2001.
- In XI and XII classes, new curriculum of vocational education was initiated. Thus, many new courses were included in the curriculum according to the demands of the economy.
- The Board introduced Bhoti languages from Class I in the Spiti sub-division of L & S District. In addition, English was introduced as a compulsory subject from Class I.
- The committee set up by the Board compared the XI and XII class syllabi with the CBSE's syllabi and introduced CBSE curriculum for XI and XII classes only for science stream from the academic year 2004 to help students of the hilly state to join the national mainstream.

(a) Curriculum Load

To reduce the curriculum load at the primary level, some steps have been taken by introducing integrated textbooks prepared and designed by the DPEP. However, as mentioned earlier from the session 2004-05 new syllabi for XI and XII Classes in science stream have been introduced as per recommendations of the academic committee of the Board. A subject expert in Mathematics and Biology suggested for preparation of course modules for XI and XII Classes for these two subjects. To cope with the increased course content load of accelerated modules for students of XII in Mathematics and Biology, the committee recommended for extra periods to complete the course within the stipulated time frame.

(b) Curriculum and Globalisation

The Board has thought regarding curriculum only in the context of national level and not at international level. Therefore, no change been incorporated in the curriculum to respond to globalisation.

(c) Vocational Curriculum

In case of vocational education, relevant areas were identified and an appropriate curriculum was designed. An expert committee developed curricula for these courses through the preparation of guidelines regarding format and content in relation to the skills to be acquired. An important consideration was that the course should be relevant and have ready marketability. Vocational courses have been blended with work education at higher secondary stage. The vocational courses introduced by the Board cater to all categories, i.e., SC/ST, girls and physically challenged students. The courses focus on life-related aspects and have more local relevance. Some of these courses are: food processing, aquaculture, trance-agency operations, computer network, consumer electronics, riverine and reservoir fisheries, hospitability, industry and business, food packaging etc.

III. Examination

The Examination Committee is an important body of the Board. The Chairman of the Board is the Chairman of Examination Committee. Other members include the secretary and three persons from amongst the Board. The Secretary of the Board acts as Secretary of the Examination Committee. The main functions of Examination Committee are conduct of examinations, certification to recommend measures to improve the mode of evaluation, and to make recommendations on matters connected with examinations.

A brief analysis of the practices to achieve these functions by the Board is given as under:

(a) Conduct of Examination

The most important functions of a Board is to conduct public examinations for students of middle, secondary and senior secondary school stages. For that, first of all the examination admission forms are serialised. The Board through the head of institutions supplies the forms for regular students free of cost. The private students get the forms from the Board office or from booksellers on payment. The form properly filled in by the candidate in his/her handwriting and duly attested by the head of the institution is sent to the Board office along with prescribed fee by the due date. The examination fees for regular and private candidates are different. The last date for receipt of applications is generally printed on the admission form.

The Board office scrutinizes the admission forms. The roll number slips with photographs of students pasted on them are sent to the students through heads of the institutions in case of regular candidates, and for private candidates these are sent directly.

(b) Examinations Conducted by the Board

The Board conducts the following examinations:

- Middle Standard examination (8th year)
- Secondary (10th year)
- Senior Secondary, Part I examination (11th year)
- Senior Secondary, Part II examination (12th year)
- Junior basic teachers, language teachers, drawing masters and certificate in physical education, oriental teachers, diploma in home science examinations, trained teachers certificate examination and pre-vocational examination.

(c) Conditions of Eligibility

There are three categories of students who appear in the examinations held by the Board:

- Regular students
- Private students
- Re-appear students

All regular students who have 75 per cent attendance are eligible to appear in the examinations. Re-appear students can appear in the subjects in which they have got compartment, during the next ensuing supplementary examinations. They are given two chances to appear in supplementary examinations.

(d) Conduct of Supplementary Examinations

In addition to the annual examination the Board conducts supplementary examinations. The supplementary examinations are governed by certain rules. The Board allows supplementary examination for secondary and senior secondary students. Earlier, the examination was held in the month of September every year. From 2001 onwards the Board gives two chances to students to appear in the supplementary examination. Sometimes, at the discretion of chairman students who are not able to clear supplementary examination in two chances may get a third chance, known as 'golden chance'.

Table 3.3: Supplementary Examinations

Year	*Secondary*		*Senior Secondary*	
	Appeared	*Passed (%)*	*Appeared*	*Passed (%)*
1998	13105	49.99	1270	56.00
1999	8376	52.65	6877	60.72
2000	20063	66.30	27156	61.21
2001	8478	58.09	6125	57.75
2002	9647	60.93	8494	55.92

Source: *Annual Reports: 2000, 2001, 2002, 2003*. H.P. Board of School Education.

Table 3.3 shows that quite a good number of students appear in the supplementary examinations and more than 50 per cent students generally pass the examination. At the secondary level their pass percentage varies from 49.99 per cent to 66.30 per cent, and at senior secondary level it varies from 55.92 to 61.21 per cent.

(e) Examination Centres

Generally the examination centres are created at different and suitable places by the examination committee of the Board. The Board creates an examination centre in a school, where there are at least 80 students. However, the centres at remote and difficult places are created even for smaller number of students under public pressure. To run examination smoothly, centre superintendents, deputy superintendents, invigilators, coordinators and assistant coordinators are appointed by the Board and Directorate of School Education. The clerk of the school, functions as assistant superintendent, in addition to clerk of the examination centre. The Class IV staff is attached to the examination centre as per practice of the Department of Education and Board. He/she is paid remuneration for the examination days by the Board. The 'book of instructions for superintendents and supervisory staff' and other important documents are supplied to each centre superintendent who has to conduct the examination efficiently and smoothly in accordance with the rules and regulations. To maintain the secrecy of the candidates, stickers are pasted on the enrolment of the candidates.

The Board conducted the first examination in 1970 at 99 examination centres. Keeping in view the increased number of candidates and typical geographical conditions of the state, the total number of examination centres during 2004, were increased to 3941, out of them 93 per cent were in rural areas. Of these, 1405 centres were for the middle, 1299 for the secondary, 621 for +1 (XI), and 616 for +2 (XII) class examination (Table 3.4).

Table 3.4: Distribution of Examination Centres

Year	*Exam*	*Rural*	*Urban*	*Total*
2000	Middle	1077	80	1157
	Secondary	939	71	1010
	Plus two	437	33	470
2001	Middle	1128	85	1213
	Secondary	1010	75	1085
	Plus one	493	37	530
	Plus two	489	37	526
2002	Middle	1160	87	1247
	Secondary	1075	81	1156
	Plus one	509	38	547
	Plus two	520	39	559
2003	Middle	1229	92	1321
	Secondary	1119	84	1203
	Plus one	550	41	591
	Plus two	540	41	581
2004	Middle	1307	98	1405
	Secondary	1208	91	1299
	Plus one	578	43	621
	Plus two	573	43	616

Source: *Annual Reports: 2000, 2001, 2002, 2003*. HP Board of School Education.

(f) Setting of Question Papers

The experienced teachers set the question papers. For each subject, three sets of question papers are made. Then they are sent to moderators.

The chairman feels that according to the merit, paper setters must be appointed. To facilitate the work, subject-expert cells in the Board needs to be set. During 2003-04, the Board had set 181 papers. The need to train paper setters in the state is also felt. But if training is given to only those paper setters who are involved in paper setting, there may be chances of malpractice. Therefore, all the paper setters on the panel need to be given training. It would involve a huge some of money.

(g) Unfair Means in Examination

The State has passed an Act, namely HP Prevention of Malpractices at University, Board or other specified examinations, to curb use of unfair means in examination. The Act provides for prevention of use of unfair means and other malpractices. If any body is found in the use of malpractices, he/she is liable to prosecution and with punishment of three months, and a fine of Rs. 2000/- or both. Though the Board is taking strict measures to stop copying in examinations, still this practice continues in the schools. The Table 3.5 shows that over the years the number of students indulging in malpractices has increased. During 1998-99, 2076 cases of unfair means were found; these increased to 2984 during 2002-03. On the other hand, the action taken against such cases also increased over the years. During 1998-99 out of 2076 cases, action was taken in 1720 cases; the gap of both was only 356 cases. But in 2002-03 out of 2984 cases, action was taken against only 2056 cases. The gap increased from 356 (1998-99) to 928 cases (2002-03), in spite of 35 meetings by the committee members to sort out the cases (see Table 3.5).

Table 3.5: Cases of Unfair Means in the Examination in HP Board

Year	*No. of Cases*	*Action Taken (No.)*	*Action not Taken (No.)*	*No. of Meetings*
1998-99	2076	1720	356	29
1999-00	3275	2903	372	25
2000-01	3177	2733	444	24
2001-02	3181	2437	744	38
2002-03	2984	2056	928	35

Source: *Annual Reports: 2000, 2001, 2002, 2003*. HP Board of School Education.

To create awareness about the evil effects of copying, the students in all schools before they take their examination, are administered an oath of sincerity and probity so that they desist from indulging in evil practice, at least on moral grounds. The Board has carved out a provision to give an ex-gratia grant of Rs. 4 lakhs to the next of the kin of any teacher/employee losing life while on examination duty to check copying, and Rs. 2.5 lakhs to those who sustain 40 per cent injuries while attempting to curb copying.

(h) Evaluation and Re-evaluation

The Board earlier followed two procedures in the process of evaluation. Either the answer books were directly sent to the examiners for evaluation or evaluation was done at the headquarters. But to expedite the work of evaluation, now the evaluation is carried out through centralised system, i.e., at the headquarters. The centralised evaluation helps in better quality of work and early declaration of results. Table 3.6 shows that the number of evaluators has increased from 3601 to 5304 (1998-99 to 2001-02), but in the next subsequent year, i.e., 2002-03, except the evaluation coordinators, the number of head examiners, sub-examiners and total evaluators decreased. One of the reasons may be that during this period the number of appeared students also declined from 140323 to 138356 in high school (in Table 3.8).

Table 3.6: Number of Evaluators in Secondary and Senior Secondary Examination, HP Board

Year	*Head Examiners*	*Sub-Examiners*	*Evaluation Coordinator*	*Total Evaluators*
1998-99	560	2975	66	3601
1999-00	539	2974	96	3609
2000-01	753	3797	170	4720
2001-02	880	4216	208	5304
2002-03	814	3681	276	4771

Source: *Annual Report: 2000, 2001, 2002, 2003*. HP Board of School Education.

With a view to maintaining transparency in functioning, the Board permits re-evaluation and re-checking of answer books. The facility of re-checking is only for Classes XI and XII. Thus, for Classes XI and XII, the answer script of the student concerned could be shown to him/her. The candidate, who feels that his/her performance has been under evaluated, may apply for re-evaluation within a prescribed time to the Board through proper channel, on the prescribed performa and depositing prescribed fee.

Table 3.7 shows that over the years, grievances against evaluation of answer sheets have increased among students. From 1998-99 to 2002-03, the total cases of re-evaluation increased from 2775 to 5637 and re-checking cases increased from 6802 to 10832. It is also found that more than 90 per cent of cases were solved. This procedure affected the result of the Board. In many cases marks of the students are increased. Because of the error on the part of an evaluator, sometime a student can lose an academic year. Therefore, need for training of evaluators is felt by the Board officials, so that re-evaluation/re-checking cases can be reduced.

Table 3.7: 'Distribution of Students' Answer Scripts for Re-evaluation and Re-checking, 1998-99 to 2002-03

Year	*Re-evaluation*		*Re-checking**	
	Total Cases	*Solved Cases*	*Total Cases*	*Solved Cases*
1998-99	2775	(100.0)	6802	6560 (96.44)
1999-00	2169	2169 (100.0)	5958	5958 (100.0)
2000-01	3807	3539 (92.96)	6251	5853 (93.63)
2001-02	3929	3906 (99.41)	7057	7770 (96.43)
2002-03	5637	4526 (97.60)	10832	10462 (96.58)

Source: *Annual Report: 2000, 2001, 2002, 2003*. HP Board of School Education.
Note: Figures in brackets indicate percentages.

(i) Evaluation and Examination Results

More than five lakh candidates appear annually in the examinations conducted by the Board.

Conducting examination is a big task that is handled meticulously by the Board. The question papers are printed centrally, and remain confidential. The parcels containing question papers are dispatched to the branches of various nationalised banks for their safe custody. On the day of the examination, the bank manager, as per the date sheet of examination, hands over the question papers to the centre superintendent. To ensure the fair conduct of examination, the Board appoints observers at almost each examination centre. Special team from headquarters also carries out random checking. But sometimes, due to human errors examinations of some classes are cancelled. For example during 1999, 12th Class English papers in Chamba centre were inadvertently distributed to 10th Class students. Therefore, examination had to be cancelled and re-examination papers were sent through Board officials.

Answer papers along with the attendance sheet are sent to the Board. The evaluation on the answer papers is organised in the Board itself.

Most of the evaluators are teachers from schools and have been trained and oriented in the marking scheme. A co-coordinator is appointed to oversee the overall procedure of the evaluation.

After computerisation of the marks, the Board declares the results within two months. The mark sheets as well as certificates are computerised. To avoid malpractice, the photographs of students are affixed on respective certificates.

(j) Declaration of Results

The declaration of results is one of the most important and difficult functions of the Board. The examinees after appearing in the examination wait very anxiously for the outcome of their performance and achievement because their future careers depend upon it. The Board started computerisation of results from 1982.

After declaration of results, it is the Board, which issues mark sheets and certificates of the students within a week. This facility helps the students, who want admission in educational institutions in other states for further education.

The Board publishes the results of middle, high school, XI, XII classes and JBT. It gives information in detail about the total number of its examinees, pass percentage, pass out students aggregate subject-wise, and sex-wise. A merit list of students who win scholarships and distinction is also prepared and published. Photographs of the students holding first position among the boys and the girls are usually announced through local leading newspapers. Results are announced through nine media, viz. Board's website, IBRS telephone facility, e-mail, *lokmitra suchana kendra*, touch screen based e-kiosks, Reliance India mobile's R-word service, SMS on BSNL and Air-tel mobile phones, newspapers and official gazettes.

(k) Students' Performance

Examination results and student's performance are indicators of the effectiveness of an educational organisation.

In the last five-years the number of students appearing both for high school and higher secondary examinations are erratic. During 1999-2000, the number of high school students appeared were 1.35 lakhs; it came down to 1.26 lakhs in 2001-02. Again in next year, the number of students appearing increased to 1.51 lakhs. In subsequent years again, the number of appeared students had a decreasing trend (Table 3.8).

Table 3.8: High and Higher Secondary School Examination Results in 1999-2000 to 2003-04

Year	*High School*		*Higher Secondary*	
	Appeared	*Passed %) (*	*Appeared*	*Passed %) (*
1999-00	1,35,524	58.86	90,083	35.63
2000-01	1,26,994	46.43	88,826	39.63
2001-02	1,51,649	48.36	78,371	42.51
2002-03	1,40,323	48.08	54,644	53.65
2003-04	1,38,356	59.94	72,479	60.54

Source: Office Records of the Board.

Similar trend was observed for higher secondary stage. During 1999-2000, 0.90 lakh students appeared in the public examination of higher secondary education. After that up to 2002-03, the number of students appeared in the Board examination decreased steadily, i.e., from 0.90 lakh to 0.54 lakh. However in 2003-04 appeared students increased to 0.72 lakh. There is a need to find out the reasons for decrease of students both at the high school as well as at the higher secondary stage. The percentage of high school students passed as against the number of students appeared for Board examination ranges between 46 and 60. The extent of successful completion of school education is better in high school than in higher secondary examinations. In higher secondary examination, pass percentage ranges from 35 to 60 per cent.

The pass percentage of students of both stages, that is, in high school examination and in higher secondary examination, girls scored better than boys, except in 2001-02 (51.55 for boys and 45.90 for girls). In high school, pass percentage of boys ranged from 30.54 to 59.98, while of girls it ranged from 45.90 per cent to 68.96 per cent. Similarly, in the higher secondary stage, boys scored less than girls in examinations. Boys' pass percentage ranged from 32.97 to 57.50, while that of girls it was between 39.56 and 64.04 (see Table 3.9).

Table 3.9: Gender-wise Pass Percentage in High School and Higher Secondary Exams in 1999-2000 to 2003-04

Year	*High School*		*Higher Secondary*	
	Boys	*Girls*	*Boys*	*Girls*
1999-00	50.28	68.96	32.97	39.56
2000-01	41.16	50.83	35.51	45.59
2001-02	51.55	45.90	38.50	47.92
2002-03	30.54	65.67	48.56	60.25
2003-04	59.98	60.07	57.50	64.04

Source: Office Records of the Board.

Financial Administration

The Finance Committee is an important body within the Board. The Chairman of the Board is the Chairman of the Finance Committee. Other members include the Secretary of the Board, officials from the Department of Education, from the office of the Secretary to the Government of HP, from the Department of Finance and two persons nominated by the Board from amongst its members.

The Secretary of the Board acts as Secretary of the Finance Committee. The Finance Committee examines the annual budget and all matters relating to the finances of the Board which are referred to it. It also scrutinizes proposals of new expenditure and advises the Board thereon.

Funding Pattern

HP Board of Education being a separate autonomous body duly constituted by an Act, it used to get grant-in-aid from the Government. It had to prepare its own budget annually and place the annual report before the HP State Legislature. But from 1998-99, the Board is not getting any financial assistance from the Government.

The sources of income of the Board are categorised as: examination fees, recognition fees, contribution from loans, royalty and charges, donations and endowments, sale of priced publications, rent and profit from property and other funds.

Table 3.10 shows that the Government's contribution is nil to the finances of the Board of School Education. The income is largely accrued from private sources, mainly from the students in the form of examination fees and sale of priced publications. The income of the Board increased from Rs. 1775.05 lakh in 2000-01 to Rs. 2345.24 lakh in 2003-04. Out of it, examination fees was 47 per cent in 2000-01 which rose to 54.97 per cent in 2003-04. On the other hand, income from sale of publications reduced from 48.06 per cent in 2000-01 to 39.56 per cent in 2003-04. Income from other sources was insignificant.

Table 3.10: HP Board Sources of Income for 2000-01 and 2003-04

	2000-01 (%)	*2003-04 (%)*
Government Grant	–	–
Examination Fees	47.0	54.97
Recognition Fees	0.81	0.82
Contributions & Loans	0.06	0.58
Royalty & Charges	–	–
Donations & Endowments	–	–
Sale of Priced Publications	48.06	39.56
Rent & Profit from Property	0.02	0.17
Other fund received	4.03	4.56
Total Income in Lakh (Rs.)	1775.05	2345.24

Source: Office Records of the Board.

Further bifurcation of examination fees shows that the Boards charges different fees for regular candidates and private candidates. Subsidies are given to SC/ST/OBC/physically challenged students.

Table 3.11 shows that the regular students' examination fees increased from Rs. 200 in 2000-01 to Rs. 210 in 2003-04 and for private students from Rs. 230 in 2000-01 to Rs. 250 in 2003-04. For higher secondary, examination fees for regular and private students respectively increased from Rs. 200 to Rs. 220 and from Rs. 250 to Rs. 270. For compartment candidates, the examination fee remained the same for high schools as well as for higher secondary schools.

Table 3.11: Examination Fee in HP Board Schools 2003-04 (in Rs)

Name of Examination	*Regular Student*		*Private Student*		*Compartment Student*	
	2000-01	*2003-04*	*2000-01*	*2003-04*	*2000-01*	*2003-04*
High School	200	210	230	250	150	150
Higher Secondary	200	220	250	270	150	150
Weaker Sections	0	0	0	0	0	0

Source: Office Records of the Board.

Table 3.12 shows that HP Board of School Education, during 1998-99, had a surplus income of Rs. 185.5 lakh. But in the next year, the Board had a deficit budget of Rs. 61.0 lakh. The reason of decline was that the Chairman of the Board refused annual grant-in-aid from the Government. The Chairman started many new programmes and courses to generate income and was successful in converting deficit budget into surplus budget within two years. Thus the Chairman made the Board a self-financing body. By the year 2002-03, the surplus budget with the Board was Rs. 1225.4 lakh.

Table 3.12: Summary of Budget (in lakhs)

Year	*Income*	*Expenditure*	*Surplus/Deficit*
1998-1999	1406.6	1221.1	+ 185.5
1999-2000	1827.0	1886.0	-61.0
2000-2001	1775.2	1805.2	-30.0
2001-2002	2548.6	1844.6	+ 704.0
2002-2003	3376.6	2149.2	+ 1225.4

Source: Office Records of the Board.

Conduct of examinations is a major task of all the Boards in terms of income and expenditure. From this account the Board is able to generate surplus budget. Table 3.13 indicates that from 2000-01 to 2003-04, there has been a steady growth in the income from examinations. It has increased from Rs. 834.41 lakhs to Rs. 1289.17 lakhs.

On the other hand, expenditure on the conduct of examinations has increased from Rs. 165.84 lakhs to Rs. 529.06 lakhs. This shows that the Board earns a good amount of surplus income under this head. During 2000-01, the surplus income was Rs. 668.57 lakhs, which increased during 2003-04 to Rs. 760.11 lakhs.

Table 3.13: Income and Expenditure on Examinations

Particulars	*2000-01*	*2003-04*
Income from Examination Fees (Rs)	83441584	128917542
Expenditure from Conduct of Examination work (Rs)	16584296	52905956
Total Surplus Income from Examination Fees (Rs)	66857286	76011586

Source: Office Records of the Board.

Table 3.14 indicates details of expenditure on the conduct of examinations. The expenditure has increased more than three times during a span of three years, i.e., from Rs. 165.84 lakhs to Rs. 529.06 lakhs in 2000-01 to that in 2003-04. Remuneration to head examiner has been increased more than three times, while that to evaluators increased almost four times. Printing cost of question papers has almost doubled. However, remuneration for paper setters has not been increased like other heads.

Table 3.14: Expenditure on Conduct of Examinations (Rs.)

Particulars	*2000-01*	*2003-04*
Remuneration for Paper Setters and Moderators	228642	374547
Remuneration to Head Examiner	6917031	22119429
Remuneration to Evaluators	5638625	23021718
Printing of Question Papers	3500000	6411879
Any other	300000	978383
Total	**16,584,298**	**52,905,956**

Interaction with the Board Officials

The aim of the School Board is to maintain and coordinate the standards of secondary education. Therefore, to understand the philosophy, working and perception about secondary education in HP, Chairman Prof B.R. Rahi and other Board officials were interviewed.

Focus of the interview was on the following issues:

- Role of the Board in improving the quality of school education and changes made in the policies and practices of the Board;
- Change need to achieve quality.

The HP Board was established to achieve excellence in bringing about academic and examination reforms in the larger interest of the students. Quality of school education depends upon three components, i.e., curriculum, instruction procedures (teaching-learning process), and evaluation. If the Board's functions are analysed in this context, it can be said that the Board has been taking measures with regard to change in the system. It succeeded because adequate measures were initiated at appropriate time. Another reason for success was the official patronage and support, including the political will.

While discussing the role of the Board in improving the quality of education the Chairman of the Board mentioned that first of all image of the Board needed to be changed from that of merely being an examination Board to that of it being an education Board. In this process, attention needed to be paid to following areas:

- Continuous and comprehensive evaluation (CCE).
- Development of co-curricular activities.
- Evaluation of course content.
- Devising of student friendly techniques of learning.
- Refresher courses for teachers.

Because of administrative problems, the Board has not initiated the scheme of CCE yet. In addition, in the evaluation process, the coverage of non-scholastic aspects of pupil development have to become an important component of the scheme of evaluation. In non-scholastic aspects, evaluation of personal and social qualities, interest, attitude, proficiency in literacy, scientific and cultural activities, etc. has not been incorporated at the secondary and senior secondary levels. Therefore, students do not pay attention to these areas as needed by them.

The interaction with officials, analysis of the documents and observation of the functioning of the Board revealed that changes in the curriculum and syllabi have been incorporated from time to time, though the entire curriculum updation for all classes has not taken place as yet. However, in some of the subjects syllabus was updated and in some subjects some new chapters were added. As far as flexibility in choice of subjects is concerned, students up to X standard have to offer all the five subjects prescribed by the Board. However, student of classes XI and XII can choose subjects as per the streams of Arts, Science or Commerce. Apart from the above subjects, a student can opt for any one vocational subject in Class XII. Vocational subject has both theory and practical examination.

The textbooks are written by experienced teachers, which are approved by the Board's Textbook Committee. When the Board was established, the textbooks were got printed through leading printers and printing paper was supplied by the Government of India to printers on subsidised rates. But later, the Board modified its policy with regard to school textbooks. The Board started publication and printing of textbooks itself and responsibility for distribution of textbooks was carried out through private booksellers apart from depots of the Boards and book co-operatives. The change in policy was made in order that the students be able to get textbooks in time.

In the case of chronic menace of 'copying', there was a phenomenal decline in the copying cases over the years in annual examinations conducted by the Board. To create awareness about the evil effects of copying, the students in various schools, before they took their examination, were administered an oath of sincerity and probity so that they could desist from indulging in this evil practice at least on moral grounds. So much so, even Gram Panchayats seeking examination centre in their areas were asked to submit an affidavit of assurance to the Board that there would be no outside interference at the examination centre located in the area of the Panchayat concerned.

In case of vocational education, relevant areas were identified and an appropriate curriculum designed. An expert committee developed the curricula for these courses through the preparation of guidelines regarding format and content in relation to the skills to be acquired. An important consideration was that the course should be relevant and should have ready marketability. Vocational courses have been integrated with work education at higher secondary stage. The vocational courses introduced by the Board cater to all categories, i.e., SC/ST, girls and physically challenged students according to local requirements. The courses focus on life-related aspects and more local relevance.

Apart from these, Information Technology (IT) courses have been introduced in the senior secondary schools. The schools running IT courses are provided with Internet connections and magazines related to the field of information technology are subscribed.

It is the first Board in the country to provide examination results of Board classes through nine mediums, viz.: the Board's website, through telephone, E-mail, *Lok Mitra Suchana Kendra,* Touch Screen Based E-Kiosks, Reliance India Mobile's R-Word Service, SMS on BSNL and Airtel Mobile Phone, newspapers and official gazettes.

With a view to maintaining transparency in the evaluation process, the Board has made provision in which an answer script of the classes XI and XII students could be shown to the concerned student. Likewise, to benefit the student, a system of re-evaluation exists for class 10th.

To avoid malpractices, in the issue of certificates, the photographs of students are affixed on their certificates.

One of the functions of the Board is to do academic reforms in the larger interest of students. It is in this backdrop, setting of a 'Student's Grievance Cell' is in the pipeline, so that members of the cell may immediately redress their grievances.

Creation of 158 new examination centres, introduction of sport evaluation in respect of XI Class from 2004 are other steps to facilitate students.

In case of examination reforms, emphasis was laid on checking the unfair means in the examination system, introduction of multiple sets of examination papers, computerisation of process of examination results, etc.

The Board has the commendable aim of venturing to provide educational access for the disadvantaged. To promote them the opportunity the Board provides the following facilities:

- Physically challenged students have option to leave the Mathematics subject and opt for any other additional subject in place of Mathematics.
- Out of three languages they can opt for one language.
- The Blind can take vocal music and instrumental music.
- Examination fee is not charged.
- Blind students get half an hour extra time in examination and there is a provision to get 'writer' in examination.

One of the functions of the Board is to grant affiliation to private schools. Every institution seeking recognition has to meet the standard requirements of building, teaching staff, equipment and other educational facilities. Where these requirements are not complied with, the authority issues notice to the concerned school. Then the control and check on private schools lies in the hands of School Board. At present, there are 1700 affiliated private schools from primary to secondary levels. Out of them, 87 were personally visited by the Chairman. In 66 of the schools, flaws were found and notices issued to them. Some school principals give false lists of teachers although they have never been appointed. To check this malpractice, photographs of teachers are to be given to the Board. In addition, every institution has to submit the certificate of fire-fighting arrangement from competent safety authority.

Recommendations

The functioning of the Board is satisfactory with reference to the relevant Act. However, following recommendations could be considered for enhancing quality and change:

- HP Board runs under the surveillance of the government and to the large extent Board has to follow the instructions of the government. Therefore, it is of paramount importance that the Board should be fully autonomous in discharging its functions and duties.
- Strong co-ordination with Directorate of Education for monitoring of school education needs to be developed.
- The need of the hour is the total personality development of children. Therefore, purpose of education is to shoulder the responsibility of judging the extent to which the multifaceted objective has been realised. In the evaluation process, the coverage of both scholastic and non-scholastic aspects, of pupil development has to become an important component of the scheme of evaluation. In non-scholastic aspects evaluation of personal and social qualities, interests, attitudes, proficiency in literacy, scientific and cultural activities, etc, needs to be incorporated.
- The Board needs to be changed from an examination Board to an education Board.
- There is a need for regular training programmes for evaluators, so that re-evaluation/re-checking cases can be reduced. Over the years grievances against evaluation of answer sheets have been increasing among students. Because of the error of evaluators, the students must not loose their academic year.
- To improve the quality of schools, training of teachers is very essential. Therefore the need is introduction of large-

scale programmes of in-service teacher education for updating their knowledge of content and up-grading their skills of objective-based teaching.

- There is need to create awareness in the students about the evil effects of copying. Though the Board is taking measures to stop the menace of copying in examination, still this practice continues in the schools. Some strict measures need to be taken.
- Need for strong research wing is felt in the Board for improving the quality of secondary education, so that functional research programmes for further improving the content and process of examinations and the practices and procedures of the Boards.
- In the present era when national boundaries are disappearing, the Board has to think regarding curriculum not only in the context of national level but also from the point of view of international level. No change has been made as yet in the curriculum to respond to globalisation.
- E-connectivity helps in having better network between the schools and the Board. There is a need to go further in this direction in a state like HP, where physical barriers exist; e-education can overcome this problem. The students of remote areas can be benefited through these programmes. Use of modern teaching aids by using interactive CDs and tele-programmes can make the teaching process easy, interesting and more interactive. Tele-classrooms can overcome the shortage of staff, where through tele-conferencing, the students of different institutions can attend the same class at the same time and can share their problems and experiences with others. Just like Andhra Pradesh, which is imparting distance education through Ku-band of satellite channels, the same can be done here to provide better interaction between students, educational institutions and the directorate to make the programme a success. The scheme must be designed keeping in view the requirements of the department, institution, Education Board, students, teachers and persons linked with the education system.

4

Board of Secondary Education Madhya Pradesh

The Board of Secondary Education, Madhya Pradesh, is a corporate body, established on 1959 with the amalgamation of Mahakhoshal and Madhya Pradesh Board by an enactment of MP Secondary Education Act, 1959, which was later replaced by MP Secondary Education Act, 1965. The Board enjoys autonomous status. It is financially not dependent upon the government.

Organisational Structure of Board

The Board of Secondary Education, MP situated in Bhopal is headed by a Chairman, who is assisted by a Secretary, an Additional Secretary, a Deputy Secretary, and the Controller of Examinations at the head quarters (see Figure 4.1). The Additional Secretary looks after academic work, Deputy Secretary looks after work related to finance and accounts, and Controller of Examination looks after all the work related to examinations. Apart from it, the Board's functioning has been decentralised through regional and divisional offices. The regional office is located at Indore while the divisional offices, seven in number, are at Bhopal, Gwalior, Sagar, Rewa, Ujjan, Indore and Jabalpur. The Board has various statutory committees, which are advisory in nature. These are: Executive Committee, Finance Committee, Curriculum Committee, Examination Committee, Subject Committee, Women's Education Committee and Scrutiny Committee. These Committees look after all the functions of the Board. A Board of Directors is constituted as per the Board's regulation. The recommendations of all the committees are placed before the 'Board of Directors'. The highest executive of the Board is the Chairman who exercises his/her duties and functions as stipulated by the Board's Act. The Board of 'Directors guide the Board. The members of the Board of Directors are Chairman, Commissioner of Public Instructions and Tribal Welfare, Director of Technical and Health Education, Sports and Youth Welfare, and Chancellor or Registrar of the university. In addition, members are also nominated by the Commissioner Public Instructions, Finance Department of Government of MP, and School Education Department.

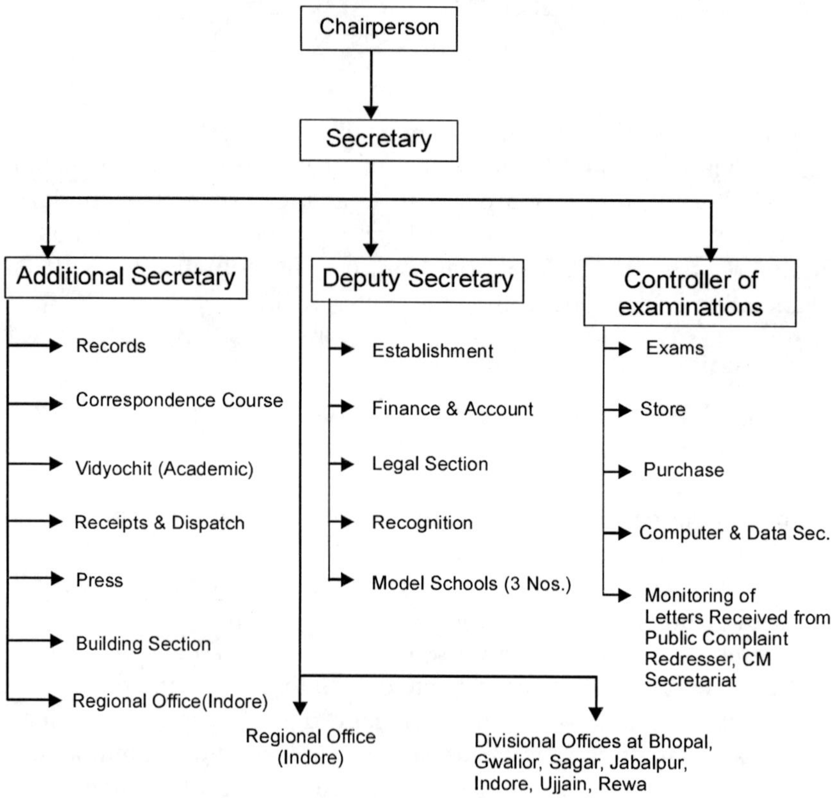

Fig. 4.1: Organisational Structure of Board of Secondary Education, MP

Functions of the Board

The study concentrates on three aspects: curriculum, instruction and evaluation process, which are concerned with quality and change in the education system. Therefore, the functions of the Board have been covering mainly these aspects. Thus the Board's main functions are:

- To take all necessary steps to promote the standard of secondary education;
- To prescribe course of instructions for secondary education, and to advise the state government for the prescription of textbooks;
- To impart teaching through correspondence course;
- To recognise educational institutions situated in MP; and
- To conduct examinations.

Decentralisation

Keeping in view the above functions, the Board has decentralised its activities. Jurisdiction of the Board extends to 48 districts in MP. There is one regional office and seven divisional officers of the Board that cater to the needs of students residing in respective areas.

Functions

The main functions of the Board can be divided into two parts (see Figure 4.2):

- Primary functions – academic, and examinations.
- Other functions – financial, administrative, and law.

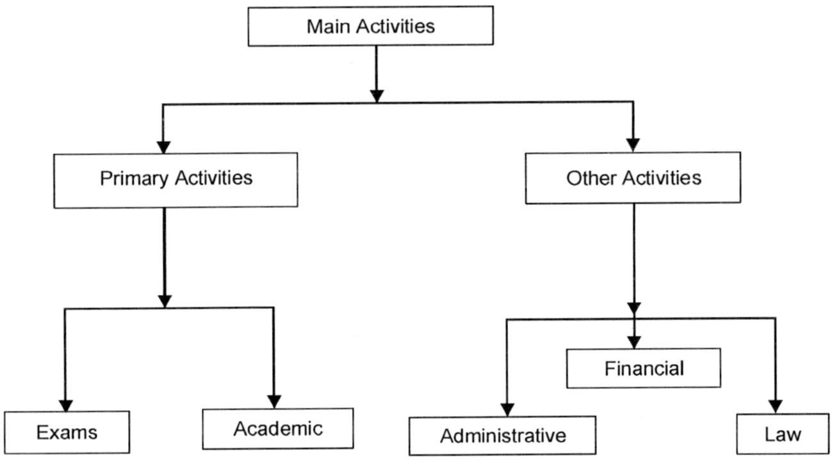

Fig. 4.2: Activities of the Board of Secondary Education, MP.

(a) Curriculum and Textbooks

The main function of the curriculum committee is to lay down syllabi and to recommend suitable textbooks. The Board has adopted curriculum for secondary school and senior secondary schools as recommended by NCERT with slight modifications. For secondary schools, textbooks for all subjects in Hindi and English medium are prescribed by the Board (English, Hindi, Sanskrit, Maths, Science and Social Science). For senior secondary schools, only books for languages are prescribed by the Board (Hindi, English and Sanskrit). For other subjects, the Board neither prepares nor recommends the textbooks.

(b) Curriculum Development and Textbook Preparation

The subject committee selects and suggests the names of eminent writers, and subject experts and from various parts of the state. Subject committee evaluates the manuscripts of the textbooks. After their proper evaluation, the Board authorities accord the final sanctions. The books are published by Madhya Pradesh Textbooks Corporation.

(c) Wide Range of Language Options

In secondary schools, the Board provides the facility to study 31 languages besides Hindi or English. Languages have two groups: special and general. In the special group, secondary school student have options of 13 languages and in general group of 18 languages. In the same way, senior secondary student can opt one language out of 12 languages in special group and in second group of 18 languages.

(d) Vocationalisation of Education

Vocational education is available at senior secondary level, i.e. at XI and XII standards. Thirty-one trades (Table 4.2) have been listed in the Board. The curriculum for vocational trades is prepared by SCERT according to the need of the region. The curriculum, after approval by the curriculum committee of the Board, is included in the syllabus of the Board examination. The particular trade to be taught in the recognised institutions, are sanctioned or allotted by the Director Public Instruction.

The Board is planning to introduce pre-vocational courses at secondary level. For this purpose, the scheme is going to be introduced on experimental basis in certain schools of District Guna.

Table 4.1 shows that from 2002 to 2003, the number of student appearing in the vocational stream is not very encouraging and that it is declining. The number of students decreased from 5784 to 5258. The reasons need to be ascertained, so that remedial measures can be taken up.

Table 4.1: Number of Students in Vocational Stream

Year	*Appeared*	*Passed*
2002	5784	4777
2003	5258	3492

Table 4.2: List of Vocational Courses for Senior Secondary School

Sl.No.	*Source Branch*	*Existing Trades (Courses) for Classes XI and XII*
1.	Agriculture	1. Agriculture Business Management
		2. Horticulture
		3. Poultry Production
		4. Dairying
		5. Repair and Management of Power Driven Farm Machinery
2.	Business and Commerce	6. Office Management
		7. Book Keeping and Accountancy
		8. Co-operative Management
		9. Steno Typing
		10. Banking Assistance
		11. Store Keeping
		12. Marketing and Salesmanship
3.	Home Science	13. Fruits and Vegetable Preservation
		14. Bakery and Confectionary
		15. Garment Making, Costume Designing and Tailoring
		16. Textile Designing
		17. Fashion Designing and Garment Making
4.	Science and Technology	18. Building Construction
		19. Repair of Radio and TV
		20. Moped, Scooter, Motorcycle Repair
		21. Repair of Electric Domestic Appliances and Electric Motor Rewinding
		22. Photography

(Contd.)

(Contd.)

Sl.No.	*Source Branch*	*Existing Trades (Courses) for Classes XI and XII*
		23. Printing, Binding and Paper Converting
		24. Computer Application
		25. Welding Technology and Fabrication
		26. Leather Technology
		27. Wooden Goods Making and Carving
5.	Health and Para Medicine	28. Hospital House Keeping
		29. X-Ray Technician
		30. Medical Laboratory Technology
		31. Auxiliary Nursing and Midwifery

Subject Combination Allowed for XII Examination

At senior secondary stage, students have three groups to choose the subjects from:

(i) Language

A student has to choose two languages in Class XII: (a) first language (special); (b) second language (general). Under the first language group, there are 13 languages and in the second language group there are 18 languages. A student has to choose one language from each group.

(ii) Diversified Subject

(a) General education courses, (b) vocational courses

The general education courses contain 6 options. Out of it the students have to offer any one course, i.e., Humanities, Science, Commerce, Agriculture, Fine Arts and Home Science.

Vocational courses have 31 trades; out of these a student can opt one trade.

(iii) The group contains (a) Socially Useful Productive Work (SUPW) or Vocational Training of a trade; (b) Physical Education or National Cadet Course (NCC), Boys Scouts and Girls Guide or co-curricular and other activities.

The subjects of this group are meant for internal examination. However, students offering Vocational Training will have the facility to appear at an examination especially conducted for the purpose and on passing it they are awarded a certificate of proficiency in the trade.

(e) Business Mathematics and Computer Applications

From 1999-2000 onward, two new subjects, i.e., Business Mathematics and Computer Applications have been added to the Humanities and Commerce group.

(f) Welfare and Multiple Growth of Students

The Board organises three types of activities for multiple growths of students and teachers:

- School magazine competition to uplift the standard of school magazines. The Board awards first, second and third prizes along with 5 consolation prizes separately to rural and urban area school magazines.
- Science exhibitions and competitions at the district and state levels, for students of rural institutions.
- Function to honour the President award winning teachers and meritorious students.

(g) Scholarships

The Board awards scholarships to the top ten position holders in secondary and senior secondary examinations. For the 1st position, Rs. 300/- pm; for 2nd position Rs. 250/- pm and for the rest 7 positions Rs. 200/- pm. The toppers in every stream in XII class examination are also awarded Rs. 250/- pm as scholarships. These scholarships are given for 2 years to the secondary school pass outs and for one year for the senior secondary pass outs.

(h) Aid to the Handicapped Students

Exemptions are provided from examination fees to the handicapped students appearing in secondary and senior secondary examinations. They are also granted an additional one and half an hour examination time apart from the normal 3 hours awarded to other students.

(i) Correspondence Course

The objective of correspondence course in MP is to provide distance education to those who are deprived of regular studies, the workingwomen and housewives. The courses educate around one-lakhs students per annum. Students are facilitated through student contact programmes. Experienced teachers provide guidance at various contact centers. Also training is provided to un-trained teachers of these courses.

(j) Model Schools by the Board

The Board runs three 'model schools' in Rewa, Bhopal and Raipur districts. The Board is responsible for their entire administration and provides full financial support. Huge amount of money is spent to run these model schools. However, these schools have set up an example of 'efficient schools' in the state.

(k) Teacher Training

To make teaching of science more effective, and to evolve curiosity among students regarding science, the Academic Division of the Board organises training for the Science and Mathematics teachers, and also for the principals of high and higher secondary schools. These orientation programmes for the teachers and the principals are organised for 10 days and 6 days respectively. In addition, the Academic Division also organises exhibition and competition of rural science children at the state and national levels. Up to 2002-03, the Board had trained 6357 such teachers.

(l) Welfare of Teachers

The Board has established a Teachers' Welfare Fund by seeking a 2 per cent voluntary contribution from teachers out of their remuneration for evaluation work. From this fund, the teachers or their dependents or the dependents of deceased teachers suffering from a calamity or major illness are being sanctioned financial assistance.

(m) Medical Facilities to Employees

The Board pays fixed medical allowance to employees. However, in case of serious illnesses, if the expenses exceed the amount of the fixed medical allowance, there is a provision for the payment of medical bills for a few special diseases.

The Board also avails the services of specialist doctors, like a cardiologist and a gynecologist. These two doctors give free consultancy to the Board employees and their families. A regular physician is also in service in the Board for general consultation.

(n) Journal Published

The Board publishes a quarterly magazine *Parikshak*, carrying exclusively essays on current problems of education in India along with directives and notifications issued by the Board from time to time. The articles published in the periodical help in the enhancement of quality of secondary education.

Examination Framework

(a) Paper-Setting Technique

Before 1995, the Board used to have a single-paper scheme, simultaneously having increased number of questions with more internal options. In view of the National Education Policy, 1986, and Programme of Action, 1992, to improve examination and evaluation system, the Board now provides multi-set question papers. For this purpose subject-wise content analysis was made and priorities of every subject were decided. Then the Board developed a blueprint of every question paper. It was decided that multiple-choice questions should be avoided. It was agreed to prepare three sets of all papers with common questions worth 20 marks.

It was also decided that while setting a question paper, care should be taken to include questions from all the three areas, i.e., Knowledge, Comprehension, Application/Skill. The format of the question paper included very short answer questions, medium short answer questions, and long answer essay type questions. The total number of each kind of questions is fixed. The places where internal options have to be put are demarcated. The subjects having maximum marks 50, should have 15 questions; those having 75 marks should have 22 questions and those having maximum 100 marks should have 30 questions.

The marking scheme is also commensurate with not only the number of questions but also with the answer contents.

(b) Continuous and Comprehensive Evaluation (CCE)

Keeping in view the large number of students appearing in the examination as well as the extensive area of Madhya Pradesh, the CCE procedure is neither possible nor manageable. However at the primary and upper primary level it is in practice.

(c) Information about Internal Assessment

Internal assessment of students is done at the school level in the form of terminal and half-yearly examinations. There is the provision of Pre-Board examination also. But marks scored in these examinations are not added in the grand total of the annual examination.

(d) Procedure for Valuation of Question Papers in Public Examinations

No sooner does the examination of a subject finish than a team of experts' analyses the question paper comprehensively. If a factual mistake or the use of ambiguous language is found, instructions for valuation, suggested by the team and duly signed by the secretary, are rushed to every valuation centre to curb any subjective element in the marking of answer-books. The Board has opted for centralised valuation supervised by the officials of the Board and under this program valuation is done at the district headquarters. Centralised valuation helps in the work to be done systematically and timely. Consequently, the students don't have to anxiously wait for a long time for their results.

(e) Rechecking/Re-valuation Facility

The number of students appearing in the examination is very large. Thus re-valuation is neither possible nor manageable. However, re-checking of marks (verification of marks) may be opted for by students. They have to fill a prescribed form in their own handwriting and submit it to the Board along with fees prescribed for it within a month of the declaration of results. The scrutiny committee verifies the marks and if it finds any question or a part of question un-valued, it gets it valued and the change in result, or no change in the result whatever may be the case, is communicated to the student within a month.

Consequent to the verification of marks, if the total of marks increases and the result of the candidate changes, then the fee deposited by him/her is refunded.

Consequent to the verification of marks, if a failed candidate makes it to the category of passed candidate, not only the fee deposited by the candidate shall be refunded, but also an amount of Rs. 500/-as a consolation amount paid to him.

(f) Number of Chances Given for Clearing a Public Examination

The students are given two chances, i.e., the annual and the supplementary to clear the examination. If a student declared eligible to appear in a supplementary examination fails there too, he/she may appear as a private candidate in a later examination. Consequently, two more chances are given to him. If he/she fails in both of them, he/she may be entertained as a student of correspondence courses run by the Board.

(g) Steps Taken for the Control of Unfair Means in Examination

In such an extensive area as Madhya Pradesh, conduction of effective and reliable examination is an uphill task. So far following steps have been taken to curb malpractice in examinations:

1. Multi-set questions-papers are used to discourage copying from one to another.
2. Close coordination is maintained with the district administration during examination time. Flying squads of the Board and District officials are constituted for surprise checks at the examination centres.
3. To ensure that students do not receive help from teachers of their own school, regular students are allotted other centres away from their own school.
4. The Board has been facing the problem of unfair means even after the completion of the examination time. Inner pages of answer copies are changed by miscreants. To counter-check this problem, the Board has changed the pattern of answer books from 2004 onwards and introduced thread-stitched copies. Secondly, from 2004, the Board is attempting a new method of collection of answer books after completion of examination time. The answer books are deposited at the nearest police station everyday. These are finally picked up at the end of all examination papers.
5. To maintain secrecy of the identity of the candidate appeared in the examinations, special 'stickers' are pasted on that portion of the answer books where the roll number is written. This is stuck on the answer books at the examination centre itself and removed only after the answer books have been valued.
6. Centres involved in mass copying in previous years are closed down and all the schools involved in mass copying are allotted centres in the Districts headquarter.
7. The names of the centres and the centre superintendents are kept strictly confidential till the last minute, to ensure that

no pre-examination 'deals' are struck between students and centre superintendents.

(h) Examination Results

The Board holds two types of examinations, i.e., secondary school certificate examination and senior secondary school certificate examination. Secondary school covers Classes IX and X and senior secondary schools cover Classes XI and XII. Two supplementary examinations, each twice in a year (March and October), is conducted by the Board.

The number of candidates appeared and passed are given in Table 4.3.

Table 4.3: Number of Candidates Appeared and Passed at Secondary and Senior Secondary Level

Year	*Secondary*		*Senior Secondary*	
	Appeared	*Passed*	*Appeared*	*Passed*
2000	736552	298591	361746	241973
2001	705699	299246	355884	246927
2002	567523	203168	312846	193027
2003	600117	147814	292868	151186
2004	656539	188381	258905	168868

Table 4.3 indicates that for secondary classes, total number of appeared and passed students declined from 2000 to 2002. After that there is a steady increase in the number of candidates. But for senior secondary classes, the declining trend continued from 2000 to 2004. The reasons may be that in 2000, Chhattisgarh state was created out of Madhya Pradesh, and that admissions to all the schools were computerised. Because of this practice, fake admissions would have stopped, specially in bordering districts schools. Earlier, fake enrolments were mentioned in the registers of the bordering district schools or interior areas of the state. After computerisation the practice of fake admissions has stopped.

Another reason may be that in senior secondary schools, two chances are given to students for clearing the public examination, i.e., the annual and the supplementary chance. If a student is declared eligible to appear in a supplementary examination and fails there too, he/she has to appear as a private candidate. Consequently, two more chances are given to him. If he/she fails in both of them, he/she may be entertained as a student of correspondence courses run by the Board. Therefore, may be because of this policy, many students are turning to correspondence courses. In correspondence courses, students get nine chances to clear the examination.

Table 4.4: Number of Regular and Private Candidates Appeared and Passed Secondary and Senior Secondary Examinations

Year	*Regular/Private*	*Appeared in Secondary Examination*	*Pass Percentage*	*Appeared in Senior Secondary Examination*	*Pass Percentage*
2001	Regular	677113	47.5	311814	77.6
	Private	28586	20.0	44070	51.0
2002	Regular	533928	39.8	265674	72.9
	Private	33595	20.4	47172	47.6
2003	Regular	573459	25.8	256648	55.4
	Private	26658	16.4	36220	36.3
2004	Regular	626866	29.1	258903	66.6
	Private	29673	18.1	N.A.	37.2

Source: MP Board of Secondary Education, Bhopal.

Table 4.4 shows that the number of regular and private students had been decreasing in schools at secondary and senior secondary levels in each successive year. At the secondary level, the number of regular students decreased from 6.77 lakhs in 2001 to 5.33 lakhs in 2002. The number of students also declined in 2003. In the same way, at senior secondary level also, the number of regular students decreased from 3.11 lakhs in 2001 to 2.58 lakhs in 2004. Almost the same trend was observed in case of private students.

Table 4.5: Examination Results: Gender-wise, 2000-2004

Year	*Secondary*				*Senior Secondary*			
	Appeared		*Passed*		*Appeared*		*Passed*	
	Boys	*Girls*	*Boys*	*Girls*	*Boys*	*Girls*	*Boys*	*Girls*
2000	498667	237885	38.30	45.23	241047	109924	62.70	76.08
2001	471347	234352	40.17	46.89	237363	118521	65.79	76.57
2002	337904	189619	37.36	40.54	208739	104107	60.01	69.03
2003	394178	205939	22.70	28.32	193873	98995	47.50	60.00
2004	426166	230373	26.70	32.40	199701	101020	57.33	68.92

Table 4.5 shows that pass percentage of girls is better than that of the boys at both the secondary and senior secondary stages. At the senior secondary stage, though the girls are performing comparatively better, yet their pass percentage had been declining every successive year from 2000 to 2004. Therefore, still improvement is needed.

Table 4.6 presents the last 16 years' results of schools of BSEMP. Two trends can be observed, one that the senior secondary school results are always better than the secondary school results; and the regular students always perform better than private students. At the secondary level, overall pass percentage is quite erratic and low. When enquired from higher authorities, they mentioned that they are taking measures to improve the quality. The schools with 0-10 per cent results are being identified after declaration of results, special stress is laid on these schools to improve their quality. One of the major problems mentioned by the Board officials is the lack of Science and Mathematics teachers in secondary schools. Schools are upgraded without increasing the infrastructure facilities and providing adequate number of teachers, specially the Science and Mathematics teachers.

Table 4.6: Results of High School/Higher Secondary (1989-2004)

Year of Exam	*Pass Percentage, Class 10th*		*Pass Percentage, Class 12th*	
	Regular	*Private*	*Regular*	*Private*
1989	43-05	23-67	77-42	51-59
1990	42-82	26-33	72-69	41-23
1991	38-91	25-15	63-01	38-53
1992	33-74	19-86	64-78	42-30
1993	44-00	34-85	58-13	39-17
1994	38-21	17-79	61-10	38-02
1995	27-96	9.80	56-59	35-99
1996	33-46	13-06	54-39	31-22
1997	38-66	17-30	58-84	34-93
1998	36-30	17-51	66-71	45-84
1999	40-59	21-51	72-15	44-86
2000	44-26	18-57	79-94	55-17
2001	47-55	20-00	77-67	51-05
2002	39-87	20-43	72-97	47-61
2003	25-88	16-43	57-86	38-12
2004	29-19	18-16	66-61	37-21

Another reason for the decline in the pass percentage is that earlier 14 grace marks were given to students in public examination by the Board. But these now have been reduced to 5. In addition, in a few districts mass copying was common in public examinations. The Board is trying hard to stop this practice. In mass copying districts, orders for videographic recording are given and if mass copying is still found, exams are cancelled.

According to the Board's directives, maximum 5 grace marks may be given in one subject or five subjects as specified below. A student is entitled to grace marks only when by awarding them the student passes the examination. A student is entitled to be accorded maximum 5 grace marks, which are divisible in the following ways:

Maximum Marks Allotted to the Question Paper	*Maximum Grace Marks*
100	05
80	04
75	04
50	03
25	01
20	01

On the basis of the maximum marks allotted to the subject, the grace marks are accorded with the clause that student has to pass separately in theory and practical. The grace marks are not added in the total marks obtained by the student in that specific subject/subjects. Only "By Grace" is stated in front of such subject/subjects.

(i) Improvement of Performance

Only one chance for division/class improvement is given to students of secondary and senior secondary. The chance has to be availed of by the student in the subsequent year and not after the expiry of that year.

(ii) Other Activities

Other activities of the Board related to finance, administration and law.

Financial Management

Matters of financial management are looked after by the Finance Department. From 2003, finance section has been computerised. The procedure for accepting the fees is totally computerised, and reconciliation of challans is being done by specially prepared computer software. In addition, accounts related cashbook is being prepared with the help of Tally software.

The functions of the Finance Department are divided into two sections:

1. Financial Management regarding examination: This section looks after reconciliation of advances to examiner centres, valuation work, honorarium payment and TA bills, etc.
2. Management of Establishment, Administration and Finance: This section prepares salary bills, makes supplementary payments, TA bills, medical, and other the payments.

(a) Sources of Income

Main sources of income of the Board are examination fees, recognition fees, enrolment fees, correspondence education fees and miscellaneous fees. The Board is not drawing any grants from the government. It generates its own resources. Thus, it maintains its functional and financial autonomy.

The classification of the Board's income was carried out taking into account the annual budget for the last five years (Table 4.7). The income is accrued from private sources mainly from the students in the form of fees, enrolment fees and recognition fees, and partly from selling the priced publications and prospectus. From 1998-99 to 2002-03, income from examination fee has increased. It was Rs. 1793.76 lakhs in 1998-99 which went up to Rs. 2577.01 lakhs in 2002-03. During the same period, income from enrolment fee has gone up from Rs. 138.66 to Rs.226.91 lakhs. However, income from recognition fee, correspondence education fee, and sale of publications and printing has declined over the five selected years. Marginal increase was observed in income from model schools run by the Board.

Table 4.7: Distribution of Sources of Income of the Board (Rs. in lakhs)

	1998-99	*1999-2000*	*2000-01*	*2001-02*	*2002-03*
Examination fee	1793.76	2339.03	2434.88	2050.69	2577.01
Enrolment ee f	138.66	161.05	164.65	198.10	226.91
Recognition fee	262.92	254.66	359.57	375.73	225.87
Correspondence Education fee	632.94	602.32	455.41	482.44	451.66
Publications	16.00	14.83	1.77	20.79	2.91
Printing	10.79	1.44	–	–	3.77
Model chools	34.59	34.90	32.08	29.26	35.43
Miscellaneous	44.35	52.54	56.78	53.35	63.08
Total	2934.01	3460.77	3505.14	3210.36	3586.64

(b) Expenditure

Expenditure by function was analysed over a five-year period. The total annual expenditure was classified as recurring and non-recurring. The recurring expenditure includes: salaries of staff, examination educational activities, correspondence education, model schools, regional and divisional offices, printing etc. Whereas the non-recurring costs comprise construction of building, purchase of vehicle, updating of learning materials, purchase of furniture, and on model schools.

Table 4.8: Distribution of Expenditure by Functions of the Board (Rs. in lakhs)

	1998-99	*1999-2000*	*2000-01*	*2001-02*	*2002-03*
Recurring Expenditure	693.17	673.68	820.24	857.23	838.72
Examination Academic Function	16.19	17.79	12.24	19.64	205.54
Model School	179.00	166.56	17.49	175.61	180.52
Salaries of the staff	1045.96	1100.57	1045.96	1066.91	1641.63
Regional & Divisional offices	389.78	404.47	428.72	332.28	275.66
Printing	309.72	389.67	464.72	332.28	275.66
Total Recurring	2723.26	2831.41	3032.10	2719.50	3414.14
Non-Recurring	191.55	49.57	127.87	88.46	139.03
Balance last year	120.66	119.93	155.00	138.96	106.64
To Expenditure	3035.47	3000.91	3314.97	2946.92	2659.81

Expenditure by functions for the year 1998-99 to 2002-03 (Table 4.8) shows that expenditure is dominated by recurring cost. The proportion of expenditure on different aspects varied for the different years, in all the five years, the highest expenditure being incurred on the salaries of staff, followed by expenditure on examination activities. Just like income, expenditure on printing had a declining trend. The expenditure declined from Rs. 309.72 lakhs in 1998-99 to Rs. 195.19 lakhs in 2002-03. The major increase in the expenditure was observed in the academic function in 2002-03. The expenditure was increased from Rs. 16.19 lakhs to Rs. 205.54 lakhs. Upto 2001-02 the expenditure on this head was only Rs. 19.64 lakhs. The academic activities contain inspection of schools, improvement in textbooks, library expenses, establishment expenses, retirement and other benefits.

Unlike other Boards, MP Board runs three Model Schools. The purpose behind setting up of Model Schools is to set an example of excellence. The Board is spending Rs. 180.52 lakhs (2002-03) on the maintenance of these schools. In comparison with the income (Rs. 35.43 lakhs) this expenditure is too high.

One of the main activities of the Board is to maintain the standards of school education. The expenditure on academic activities shows that very meager amount is spent on inspection of schools and improvement of textbooks. Even the amount spent on Board's library is very insufficient and has a declining trend. Whatever amount is spent on this head is mainly on examination system reforms, analysis of examination, remuneration of writers, scholarship, etc. During 2002-03, for first time to improve the efficiency of schools, donation to excellent schools was given by the Board (Rs. 198.00 lakhs). Earlier from 1998-99 to 2001-02, the amount on this head ranged from Rs. 12.19 lakhs to Rs. 19.49 lakhs (see Table 4.9).

Table 4.9: Expenditure of Academic Activities (Rs. in lakhs)

Academic Activities	*1998-99*	*1999-2000*	*2000-01*	*2001-02*	*2002-03*
Inspection of Schools	0.09	0.28	0.12	0.10	0.11
Improvement of text-books	–	0.06	–	0.04	0.07
Library of the Board	0.19	0.03	0.03	0.01	0.01
Establishment expenses	1.40	0.06	–	–	–
Retirement benefits	0.12	0.01	–	–	–
Others	14.39*	17.35	12.19	19.49	205.35**
Total	16.19	17.79	12.24	19.64	205.54

* Seminar expenses, curriculum improvement, examiners training, training of teachers, scholarships

** Donation to schools of excellence (Rs.198.00 lakhs) and Seminar expenses, curriculum improvement, examiners' training, training of teachers, scholarships.

Table 4.10 gives the details of expenditure on examination and valuation. Under this head, expenditure is made mainly on examination work and valuation centre. For examination work and valuation centre, the amount is spent for remuneration to administration, examiners, valuators, and on examination centres. During 1998-99, Rs. 436.03 lakhs were spent on exam and valuation centres, which increased to Rs. 628.62 lakhs during 2002-03. For data processing and computer expenses (results processing, stationary, remuneration to data entry operators, computer system and software development etc), the Board during 1998-99 spent Rs. 95.85 lakhs, which decreased after five years to Rs. 91.67 lakhs in 2002-03. In the same way, miscellaneous expenditure has also shown a declining trend. This head contains expenses on TA/DA to paper setters and valuators.

Table 4.10: Expenditure on Examination and Valuation (Rs. in lakhs)

Particulars	*1998-99*	*1999-2000*	*2000-01*	*2001-02*	*2002-03*
Expenditure on question papers	–	–	–	101.12	50.18
Exam & Evaluation centres	436.03	460.58	612.61	609.58	628.62
Miscellaneous exam expenses	161.29	120.02	95.61	44.97	46.22
Data processing & computer expenses	95.85	93.08	79.87	72.63	91.67
Establishment expenses	10.04	10.81	11.02	26.29	20.18
Retirement & other benefits	1.63	4.46	3.39	2.75	1.85

The comparative picture of income and expenditure shows that though Board is a self-financing body, even then it has surplus income from 1998-99 to 2002-03. The surplus income is used by the Board to give benefit to students and employees. Meritorious students are given scholarships out of this fund. In addition, the Board's employees earlier did not have pension scheme. The Board provides this benefit to their employees from the earning of Board (see Table 4.11).

Table 4.11: Comparative Picture of Income and Expenditure Distribution in the Board (Rs. in lakhs)

Year	*Income*	*Expenditure*	*Surplus/Deficit*
1998-99	3236.39	3035.47	+ 200.92
1999-2000	3803.55	3000.91	+ 802.64
2000-01	3934.60	3314.97	+ 019.63
2001-02	3568.06	2946.92	+ 621.14
2002-03	3996.92	3659.81	+ 337.11

Interaction with the Board Officials

School Boards were established with the aim of maintenance and coordination of secondary education. Therefore, to know the perceptions of the Board officials about secondary education, structured interview schedule was carried out. The focus of the interview was on the following issues:

- Role in improving the quality of secondary education.
- Change needed to achieve quality.

In MP Board, following persons were interviewed:

- Chairman, Board of Secondary Education: Mrs. Shashi Jain
- Secretary, Board of Secondary Education: Shri J.N. Malpani
- Academic Registrar: Shri J.L. Dube
- Personnel Relation Officer: Mr. Chorasia
- Director Training: Shri A.K. Danayak
- Chief System Officer: Shri Ashish Saraf
- Deputy Director: Shri Uma Kant Pandey
- Assistant Prof. (Home Science) and Coordinator Diploma in Education: Mrs. D.K. Bhatia

The perceptions of the officials about the functioning of the Board are as follows:

(a) Role of Board In Improving the Quality of Secondary Education

The functions of the Board that lead to quality and bring change in the system are in the areas of curriculum development, teaching-learning process and conduct of examinations.

With regard to curriculum development, the Board has adopted NCERT's curricula with slight modifications at secondary and senior secondary stages. Curriculum Development Committee looks after the curriculum development work. They select eminent writers from various parts of the state to update the curriculum. Subject Committee evaluates the manuscripts of the textbooks. After proper evaluation, the Board gives final approval. Recently, at the senior secondary stage, two new subjects have been added in the curriculum, i.e., Business Mathematics and Computer Applications. With regard to vocational education at the secondary stage Board is planning to introduce pre-vocational courses. And at the senior secondary stage, according to needs of the region, 31 trades have been included in the curriculum.

The Board publishes a quarterly journal *Parikshak* which gives inputs to teachers and related people, regarding current problems of education along with directives, notifications issued by the Board. The articles published in it help in enhancement of quality of secondary education. The Board also brings out special issues on new curriculum and results of secondary and higher secondary examinations. Before Board examination, proper guidance is given to students and parents. In addition, the Board has implemented web enabled system for: (a) disseminating information on results to students; (b) providing roll number information; (c) providing information about examination centres; (d) scrutiny of results is provided through the website of the Board. This has greatly benefited all the students, specially the ones who live in far off locations. The results of Board exams of secondary are also transmitted through web as soon as these are declared.

The Board officials think that the primary work of the Board is to conduct examinations of secondary and senior secondary levels. According to them examination results are best indicators of effectiveness of schools. How schools are functioning, and how teachers are teaching in schools can be judged by the examination results. As stated in the journal of the Board *Parikshak* by the Secretary that from last number of years, Board results have not been satisfactory. The reasons are lack of teachers; teachers are not taking adequate pains for their students; students are losing interest in studies, and cheating in the examinations has increased. Therefore, school authorities have to take adequate steps to enhance the quality of schools. The Board has started analysing the results of schools and a list of schools with 0-20 per cent results is sent to DPI to take the necessary action or to find the reasons for poor performance of schools.

During discussions with the officials of the Board, they mentioned several reasons for the bad results of the students: (a) Most of the secondary schools are upgraded from middle schools, but neither infrastructure facilities nor teachers have been provided according to the need of these upgraded schools. Teachers who were teaching in middle classes now are given responsibility to take secondary classes. As such, they are not able to do full justice. (b) Teachers who are posted in villages do not get proper housing facilities. Therefore, they live in far off places, and most of the time they are absent. (c) Teachers are not posted in schools according to the requirements; in some schools there are two teachers for seven classes and in some easily assessable areas schools have surplus teachers. (d) Teachers are given other responsibilities like duty in elections and pulse polio, help in village development plans etc. that hamper teaching in schools.

Another problem flourishing in the Board's examinations is copying. To control copying, flying squads of the Board and District officials are constituted for surprise checks at the exam centres, and to identify and close down mass copying examination centres. Special visits by officers and other inspecting officers are conducted during examination. There is a provision of certain punitive action for certain wrong doings and accordingly punishment is given.

In addition, to stop the malpractice in the examination, the Board has taken several other steps. For example, to maintain total secrecy of the identity of the candidate appearing in the examination, special stickers are pasted on that portion of the answer books where the roll number is written; introduction of thread stitched answer books have been introduced to check the problem of changing inner pages of the answer books by miscreants; the names of the centres and to which centre a particular superintendent has been appointed, are being kept strictly confidential till last minute. This ensures that no pre-examination 'deals' are struck between students and centre superintendents.

However, the quality of secondary education to a large extent depends on the quality of teaching-learning process, and the quality of aids and support to facilitate learning. To improve the teaching-learning process, the Board imparts training to teachers as well as principals. The training is imparted by Academic Section of the Board. Especially Science and Mathematics teachers are called for training. The output is very encouraging. However, monitoring of teaching-learning process is under the control of Directorate of Education. The Board also organises science fairs and similar developmental programmes with the wider involvement and participation of the learners in schools and the community.

To improve the internal efficiency of the Board, computerisation and streamlining of the system, including inventory management, accounts and payroll, has been initiated and is being continuously updated. A system of networking and a complete Management Information System to facilitate decision making on emerging functions of the Board are landmarks in the Board's governance.

(b) Changes Expected for Betterment of Quality

There is need to impart training to Board officials so that they can think about the betterment of Board also, apart from being an examining body only. They have the impression that their main function is to conduct examinations. The Board officials are busy whole year in the preparation of exams or in the results of exams. They hardly are able to think of any change in the system regarding improvement of quality of secondary education. In the name of library, only two almirahs with school magazines or school textbooks, or reference books, are kept that too in visitors waiting room attached to the Chairman's room. Need is to strengthen the library of the Board as well as the research activities. Action research projects can be taken up by Academic Unit of the Board, and research projects can be delegated to teachers for improvement of quality of education. The results of research projects would definitely change the mindset of the Board officials as well as teachers.

Strong linkage is needed with Director Public Instruction (DPI), SCERT, Madrasa Board, Open Schools, Colleges of Education or other educational organisations. The coordination would strengthen the Board's working, which would lead to necessary steps for promoting the standard of secondary education.

Good initiative has been taken up by the Board to introduce pre-vocational courses at secondary stage. But if we look at the enrolment at senior secondary stage it shows that number of students appearing in the vocational courses are decreasing over the years. There is need to find out the reasons, so that remedial measures can be taken up for pre-vocational courses at secondary stage.

The pattern of expenditure of an organisation shows the priorities of that organisation. The analysis of Board's expenditure indicates that most of the expenditure is either on salaries of the staff, examination activities or on non-recurring activities like construction of buildings or purchase of vehicles. No budget has been spent on improvement or promotion of standard of secondary education. Even excess budget is spent on Board's employees welfare fund. Therefore, need is to strengthen the research cell and research activities for improvement of quality of secondary education.

In addition there is a great need to orient the paper setters and moderators in terms of setting of quality papers.

5

School Education Boards in West Bengal

The total span of school education in West Bengal is divided into three stages, namely primary (I-V), secondary (VI-X) and senior secondary (XI-XII). All the academic matters, like framing of curricula and syllabi, preparing or approving/recommending textbooks, holding of public examinations and publishing results, are entrusted to three separate autonomous Boards for Primary, Secondary and Higher Secondary levels of education. Apart from these Boards, there are two more Boards, namely West Bengal Board of Madrasah Education, and Rabindra Mukta Vidyalaya. These two Boards also enjoy autonomous status. The Madrasahs impart education to educationally backward communities irrespective of religion, caste, creed and gender. The Madrasahs, founded with the donations of the local Muslim population, in course of time have come under the Government control. Rabindra Mukta Vidyalaya aims to impart education to the people who could not avail the opportunity at their proper age.

West Bengal Board of Secondary Education

West Bengal Board of Secondary Education owes its origin from the West Bengal Secondary Education Act, 1963, amended from time to time. The Board is an autonomous body and its decisions on academic matters do not require State Government's approval. It is supposed to advise the State Government on all matters relating to secondary education, and to lay down the general policy for development of secondary education in West Bengal among others.

Functions of the Board

Broadly the Board of Secondary Education performs functions in regard to areas such as (a) Academic, (b) Examination, and (c) Research and Development, besides management and financial matters. Subject to the provisions of the Act, the Board exercises powers and functions as below:

- Preparation of syllabi and review thereof;
- Publication of textbooks for Classes VI-X;
- To appoint committees of experts to advise on the syllabus etc. for the different courses of study;
- To frame courses of study on the recommendations of expert committees that may be appointed for the purpose;
- To arrange for the in-service training and orientation of secondary school teachers.
- Holding secondary school examinations including publication of results of both regular and external candidates and issue of certificates, publication of merit list and felicitation of meritorious students of out-standing performance in the examinations;
- To draw up panels of question paper setters, examiners etc.;
- To frame rules prescribing the minimum condition for selection of examiners, etc. and generally to frame such other rules as may be necessary for its effective functioning;
- Granting or refusing recognition to institutions; and
- Withdrawing recognition granted to institutions after considering the recommendations of the Recognition Committee.

Constitution

All the above functions of the Board are undertaken through the following committees:

- Executive Committee
- Examination Committee
- Finance Committee
- Recognition Committee
- Syllabus Committee
- Appeal Committee

Thrust Areas

Curriculum and Text-books Preparation

At the secondary level, West Bengal Board of Secondary Education (WBBSE) designs and prescribes curricula and syllabi. As per the Board authorities, the curricular revision from time to time is very essential to meet the changing requirements of the society and the nation. It has to be a continuous process. In case of WBBSE, it was overdue because the last revision was made in 1981. After almost twenty years curriculum was updated. The President mentioned that principal objectives to review the curricula is to shift the emphasis altogether from cramming to learning, and from teacher-centred courses to learner-centred ones.

At present, the Board prepares 46 textbooks. The responsibility of publishing some of the books has been entrusted to private publishers, with the condition that price, number of pages, pictures, charts, lines per page, paper quality, size of books, etc will be decided by the Board. Private publishers cannot increase the number of pages on their own. The reason for fixing the number of pages is because many publishing houses are in the habit of violating the rules and norms prescribed by the Board. In many cases, volume of the book becomes the cause of panic for students, as the prescribed syllabi are artificially and unnecessarily made to appear much heavier than they actually are. Further, differences of information and data presented in different books create confusion among the students. The Board controls the prices of the textbooks. The price of each book ranges between Rs. 18 to 27.

Quality has always been the main focus while publishing school textbooks. The Board is now using four-colour cover, with DTP printing and maplitho paper for its textbooks.

Range of Language Options

At the secondary stage, three-language formula has been adopted with some modification. The first language and English are the compulsory, second language, are taught from Classes VI to X. In addition, a compulsory third language is included in the curriculum for Classes VII and VIII. Students may choose their third language from a list of several Indian and foreign languages.

For the first language, the WBBSE offers a wide choice. As many as 17 languages are approved in this category. Students with English as their first language are required to select their second language from a list approved by the WBBSE. In Classes IX and X, the third language is dropped, but there is provision for an additional optional subject. The list of such subjects includes, among others, and the languages are noted below:

1. A-level languages – Bengali, English, Hindi, Nepali, and Urdu
2. B-level languages – Bengali, Sanskrit, Pali, Persian, Arabic, Latin, Greek, Classical Tibetan, French, German, Russian, Hindi, Portuguese, Spanish, Italian, Nepali, Classical Armenian.

For the secondary examination, the first language consists of two papers of 100 marks each. For the other languages the load is limited to one paper carrying 100 marks.

Vocational Education

Since the colonial period, various Commissions and Committees have suggested introduction of vocational courses at the secondary and senior secondary levels. These include Hartog Committee, the Wardha Scheme of Mahatma Gandhi, Mudaliar Commission (1952-53), the Kothari Commission (1964-66), and Ashok Mitra Commission (1992). Ashok Mitra Commission mentioned that about 250000 children drop out of the educational track (page 146) each year between Classes VII to X. The Commission suggested for facilitating the number of options for self-employment or vocational training or pursuit of further general education. The Kothari Commission provided three cut points: (1) after Class VIII, (2) after Class X, and (3) after Class XII. With minor modifications, the structure of Kothari Commission recommendations has been introduced in the West Bengal. At the terminal point of Class VIII, opportunity for vocational education is created in the Industrial Training Institutes. After Class X, vocational training can be had in polytechnics.

The curricular structure has been designed keeping in view the character and objective of secondary education. As the secondary education is the terminal stage of mass education, the core subjects, therefore, are compulsory for all students. However, there are a large number of students who leave school after the secondary stage and join the world of work as unskilled labour or manage some kind of self-employment. To meet their requirements, pre-vocational courses have been included at the secondary level. But these courses are optional and additional than core subjects. Whatever marks a student scores in this additional subject, 34 marks are deducted and the rest are added in the total marks of the student scored in the secondary school examination.

Decentralisation

Keeping in view the large number of students at the secondary level, the Board has decentralised its activities; jurisdiction of Board extends to 18 districts. There are 4 regional offices, which cater to the needs of students residing in those areas.

School Session

Earlier, the school session in West Bengal used to be from January-December. Later it was changed to May-April, with the objectives to bring it in line with the national pattern. At the secondary level, the total learning days are 210 days where external examinations are not held, 200 days where one external examination is held, and where two external examinations are held the number of learning days is 190 days.

Examination Fees

From 1995-96 to 2000-01, examination fees were gradually increased from Rs. 34 to Rs. 155 for regular students. For private students, the hike in examination fees was from Rs. 70 to Rs. 500. Out of Rs. 500, Rs. 300 is examination fee and Rs. 200 is for those who pass the exam, and have to pay it later. Two types of re-evaluation fees are also charged from the students who want their answer scripts to be re-evaluated. Re-valuation consists of Post Publication Security (PPS) and Post Publication Review (PPR). Fees for PPR and PPS are Rs. 40 and Rs. 50 per subject, respectively.

Recruitment of Teachers

Quality of schools generally depends upon teaching-learning process. The teaching-learning process to a great extent depends upon the quality of teachers. The West Bengal School Service Commission Act, 1977, was enacted for the purpose of recruitment of teachers, including principals of secondary schools and superintendents of senior madrasahs. The School Service Commission has its offices in four regions: north, south, east and west. Through School Service

Commission, not only qualitative recruitment of teachers at the secondary level has been made possible but the time lag between the occurrence of vacancy and its filling up has been shortened.

Teacher-Pupil Ratio

Much of the success in attaining quality in education depends on the teacher-pupil ratio. Table 5.1 shows that T/P ratio is increasing at a very fast rate. It increased from 28 in 1980-81 to 41 in 1998-99. This is because of tremendous increase in the enrolment.

Table 5.1: Teacher-Pupil Ratio

Year	*Teacher Pupil Ratio*
1970-71	28
1980-81	28
1998-99	41

Source: WBBSE

Teacher Training

To improve the quality of teachers and their teaching, the Board organises camps for in-service secondary school teachers in every district of West Bengal.

Publication of Journal

Board publishes a monthly Journal *Parshad Varta*. The journal has been very popular with teachers and students as it contains various teaching-learning material and Board's circulars. It is an effective bridge as it links schools situated in the remotest areas of the state with the office of the Board at the headquarters.

School Cluster

Right from the 1960s, a new re-organisation scheme of school education, 'School Cluster', was started in the state. These school clusters are of immense value, because these play a positive role in mobilising and sharing resources, coordinating academic and extra academic programmes, decentralising examination service and activity based learning. A new setup was created at Banipur in North 24 Parganas, Kalanabagram at Burdwan and another one at Santiniketan, Birbhum. Moreover, the SCERT, West Bengal, took up this project in some districts in collaboration with NCERT. But the concept of school cluster was not implemented as an ideal principle that senior secondary school will be playing a new role of 'Lead School'. But because of problem of coordination and sharing satisfactorily, overall acceptance of this scheme has not been taken up seriously. One or two private initiatives somehow survive with lack of support from state organisation. From 2004-05 again this scheme is started and all the schools are divided into school clusters.

Curriculum in X Class

In WBBSE, total syllabi for Classes IX and X are taken as composite units for the final examination. According to officials of the Board, examination based on broader syllabi equip the students better to meet the challenges of life.

Non-Scholastic Subjects

Physical Education

Till mid 1990s, Work Education, Physical Education, Social Service were considered as compulsory subjects for the final examination. From 1996, these have been shifted to the list of additional optional subjects. The Board found it difficult to arrange proper evaluation of these non-scholastic subjects.

Introduction of Computer Application, Computer Literacy

The Board has introduced computer education as an optional subject for Classes IX and X. About 195 schools have taken up 'Computer Application' as an additional subject. Board also conducts computer literacy programmes.

Examination

Examination Committee looks after the work related to examinations. Since 1974, four Regional Examination Councils, namely North Bengal, Burdwan, Midnapur and Kolkata were established. The reason for decentralisation was the increased workload and it was in the interest of students, teachers and guardians.

The main activities of Regional Examination Councils are:

- Processing of registration forms of the students reading in Class IX;
- Correction of mark-sheets/certificates and receiving and processing forms (subject-wise);

- Appointment of custodian and officer in-charge of examination centres of secondary education;
- Correction of registration certificates, distribution of admit cards;
- Formation of visiting team and selection of Board's nominees for the examination centres of secondary education;
- Change of centre for the candidates as per rule; and
- Preparation of centre-wise list of students.

Function of the Examination Committee

Examination section, headed by DS (Exam), is the epicentre of all activities of the West Bengal Board of Secondary Education. The Examination Committee takes policy decision in respect of examinations. During 2002-03, 8 meetings were held for arrangements for conducting examination of 5.91 lakh candidates (regular and private). Results of these candidates also were published in time.

To carry out the above functions successfully, the Board gets co-operation from railways and postal authorities, the Education Department and Directorates, Board members, the Teachers' Organisations, the respective school administrations, the teaching community in general, officers and members of the staff of the Board, and all other concerned.

Unfair Means in Examination

To control malpractice in examinations, Malpractice Committee has been formed in the Board. The members of this committee are a retired judge, two teachers and Board officials. But very few cases of malpractice were generally found.

Evaluation Process

To hide the identity of students in the examinations, Roll Numbers assigned to students are of special category. The Roll Number is of 10 digits. First three digits indicate the district code, next three digits the institute's code, next two digits the stream and the last two digits the gender of students, i.e., boy or girl. Every year the code digits are changed to maintain the secrecy.

Re-evaluation

Re-evaluation of answer scripts is done in two ways, i.e., Post-Publication Review, and Post-Publication Scrutiny. Cases of Post-

Publication Scrutiny are less than 2 per cent. In it, generally, student's pass percentage is 70 per cent.

Examination Centres

To conduct the stupendous task of holding examinations every year, WBBSE has to increase the number of examination centres keeping in view the increased number of candidates and the geographical conditions of the state. During 2000, there were 852 examination centres which increased to 912 during 2004 (Table 5.2).

Table 5.2: Distribution of Centres of Examination

Year	*Examination Centre*
2000	852
2001	892
2002	881
2003	899
2004	912

Source: WBBSE

Question Paper Setters

Experienced teachers are engaged to set the question papers. For each subjects, 3 sets of question papers are assembled. Then the answer papers are sent to moderators. During 2000, there were 78 paper setters; these increased to 81 in 2003. In the same way, the number of moderators has increased from 49 to 56 (Table 5.3).

Table 5.3: Number of Paper Setters and Moderators

Year	*Paper Setters*	*Moderators*	*Total*
2001	78	49	127
2002	78	49	127
2003	81	56	137

Source: WBBSE

Table 5.4 shows the examination results for the last eight years. It shows that as the number of appeared students in secondary examination increased, pass percentage also increased. From 1996 to 2003, the number of appeared students increased from 468641 to

580063. The Table also indicates that from 1996 to 2001, pass percentage of regular students had an increasing trend.

Table 5.4: Number of Students Appeared and Passed at Secondary Level

Year	*Appeared*	*Total Pass %*	*Pass % of Regular Student*
1996	468641	56.60	65.33
1997	472665	58.31	68.15
1998	499390	61.38	68.47
1999	529329	61.86	68.47
2000	548270	63.27	70.45
2001	564775	62.54	N.A.
2002	575833	64.75	N.A.
2003	580063	65.14	N.A.

Source: WBBSE

Table 5.5 shows that in the secondary examination, boys' pass percentage was better than that of girls'. Though boys' pass percentage was erratic during 1999 to 2003, girls were showing better performance in Board's examination every year. Their pass percentage had an increasing trend from 1997 to 2003, except in 2001.

Table 5.5: Gender-Wise Students Appeared and Passed

Year	*Appeared*		*Passed*			
	Boys	*Girls*	*Boys*	*%*	*Girls*	*%*
1997	236185	190814	149785	63.42	105652	55.37
1998	296506	202884	188085	63.43	118448	58.38
1999	329925	219265	198652	60.21	128817	58.75
2000	318141	230129	207473	65.21	139440	60.59
2001	327834	236941	211845	64.62	141368	59.66
2002	327025	248808	223573	68.36	149275	60.00
2003	323492	256571	219917	67.98	157946	61.56

Source: WBBSE

Finance

In all organisations, Finance section holds a key position. The section looks after the resources to balance the receipts and expenditure. Board is largely dependent on the grant from the State Government to meet the expenditure for conducting examinations, for payment of salary to staff and other activities. To augment resources, the examination fees were increased from Rs. 35 to Rs. 155 for regular candidates and from Rs. 60 to Rs. 500 for the external candidates. According to the Board officials the increase is insignificant with respect to actual expenditure incurred for the purpose.

The sources of income for WBBSE are grants from the government, examination fees, royalty and charges, donations and endowments, interest on sale and purchase of land and other funds. Table 5.6 shows that during the six years from 1995-96 to 2001-02 income of the Board had almost doubled. It increased from Rs. 1270.02 to Rs. 2348.59 lakhs. But in terms of percentage income, it decreased for all the heads of expenditure, except for examination fees. The examination fees had increased from 13.32 per cent to 36.29 per cent during the selected period.

Table 5.6: Sources of Income (Rs. in Lakhs)

Particulars	*1995-96*	*%*	*2001-02*	*%*
Grants from Government	493.00	38.82	886.16	37.73
Examination fees	169.18	13.32	852.30	36.29
Royalty & charges	–	–	1.44	0.06
Donations & Endowments	0.17	0.01		
Interest on sale & purchase of land	9.47	0.75	16.82	0.72
Other funds received	598.20	47.10	591.87	25.20
Total	1270.0	100.00	2348.59	100.00

Source: WBBSE

Expenditure

Table 5.7 shows that Board expenditure on staff salary increased more than two times and for examination work also expenditure increased. For publications and development, the expenditure has declined from 1995-96 to 2001-02.

Table 5.7: Items of Expenditure (Rs. in Lakhs)

Particulars	*1995-96*	*2001-02*
Staff Salary	360.49	841.09
Examination Work	306.79	594.69
Publications	422.39	317.43
Development Expenditure	2.18	1.90

Source: WBBSE

Table 5.8 shows that from 1995-96 to 2001-02, expenditure on printing of question papers increased to more than double, while expenditure on paper setters, moderators, evaluators and other expenditure has decreased.

Table 5.8: Expenditure on Conduct of Examination (Rs. in lakhs)

Items	*1995-96*	*%*	*2001-02*	*%*
Expenditure to paper setters, moderators, evaluators	97.83	27.11	154.16	25.92
Printing of question papers	60.36	16.73	227.48	38.25
Any other	148.60	41.19	213.05	35.82
Total	360.79	–	594.69	–

Source: WBBSE

Interaction with the Board Officials

The Board officials, President Shri Dibyendu Hota, Head Syllabus Committee, Head Finance Committee and Head Executive Committee were interviewed through structured interview scheduled to get their perceptions on the working of the Board, and their efforts for improvement and maintenance of secondary education.

Role of Board in the Context of Quality

The Board is supposed to advise the State Government on all matters relating to secondary education, and to lay down the general policy for development of secondary education. It is also intent upon providing quality education to all the learners. To enhance the quality following changes are made from time to time as mentioned by the Board officials:

- The schools are constantly supervised by the Board officers and members and also by the inspecting officers of the government.
- A wide range of language options are provided to students at the secondary level.
- There are a large number of students who leave school after the secondary stage and join the world of work as unskilled labour or manage some kind of self-employment. To meet their requirements, pre-vocational courses have been included at the secondary level.

- Qualitative recruitment of teachers through School Service Commission (SSC) is made possible at the secondary level. SSC has shortened the time lag between the occurrence of vacancy and it's filling up.
- To raise the quality of teaching-learning in schools and overall performance of students, recently a project was undertaken to ascertain the achievement level of schools in the secondary examination.
- Regular in-service orientation of teachers of all levels is being conducted in alliance with the SCERT, West Bengal.
- Publication of a monthly journal links schools situated in the remotest areas of the state with the office of the Board at the headquarters.
- Four regional offices were opened to facilitate students of far flung or hilly regions.
- Some significant reforms have been introduced in the examination process as:
  - (a) To avoid malpractice in the examination special category of roll numbers are developed by Board officials;
  - (b) Issuing the mark sheets and certificates of secondary examination on the date of publication of result;
  - (c) Decentralisation of evaluation system;
  - (d) Holding of work education, physical education, social service examination before the written examination of compulsory papers;
  - (e) Provision for awarding division to compartmental candidates after taking into account previous pass marks in other subjects; and
  - (f) Provision of review and scrutiny after publication of secondary results.
  - (g) The Board publishes photos of students in news papers who secure top marks in their respective subjects in the Board's public examinations.

Recommendations

Examination Reforms

The Board officials perceived quality as achievement of objectives set in the textbooks, syllabi, and by taking examinations. But the fact is, quality of secondary education is equally related to the teaching-learning process. Monitoring of teaching-learning process does not come under the purview of the Board; it lies with the Directorate of School Education. There is need of coordination between the two on this matter. Monitoring (inspection and supervision) of teaching-learning process is left with the inspectors. They are mostly busy with administrative work or court cases (Survey of Educational Administration, 2000), and hardly get time for inspection and supervision. Looking at the large number of schools and the time available with them, it becomes impossible for them to visit every school in a year.

Strengthening Teacher Education

Teacher occupies pivotal position in the system of education. For strengthening teacher education programmes, there is a need to establish linkages and coordination with other State Departments like SCERT, Primary Teachers Training Institutes (PTTIs), B.Ed. Colleges, Institutes of Advance studies in Education (IASE) and University Departments of Education. The resources human or physical, need to be shared.

Globalisation Issues

There is a need to include in the school curriculum, issues of globalisation and internationalisation as national boundaries are becoming soft. The Board must take up these challenges. While they should come forward to help the national efforts, they must also think of the ways and means to absorb the changes that will soon come in the context of changing national perspective. They should keep themselves ready in advance.

Research Wing

There is a need of research wing in the Board so that changes in the system, curricula, and syllabi can be implemented well in time. The research wing is expected to collect, summarise and publish various kinds of educational experiences in and outside the country. It will generate public awareness about national education as well as educational map of the world.

Merit List

The Board publishes every year a list of 20-30 students who have topped the list of successful candidates. Research evidence indicates the students occupying the first three to five hundred places are all equally good. It is a matter of coincidence that a few students occupy the first twenty positions. This process encourages a few students, but discourages a much larger number of students.

In the process of choosing best students only academic performance is taken into consideration leaving aside the non-scholastic achievements. The students, who are doing well in academics, may be not the best in non-scholastic achievements. The aim of examination should be to provide accurate estimate of student's performance. Therefore, instead of practice of publishing merit list be a provision for National Scholarships may be started for few hundred students.

West Bengal Council of Higher Secondary Education

History of the Council

With a view to restructuring the pattern of secondary education in the State in consonance with the All India Pattern of Secondary Education, i.e., 10+2, the state Government established the West Bengal Council of Higher Secondary Education under the West Bengal Council of Higher Secondary Act, 1975.

Autonomy and Governance

The Council is an autonomous body and has the power to direct, supervise and control higher secondary education in the State. It is fully financed by the State Government.

Functions of the Council

- To advise the State Government on all maters relating to Higher Secondary Education;
- To conduct Higher Secondary examinations;
- To prescribe course of instruction for Higher Secondary Education;
- To recognise educational institutions situated in West Bengal; and
- To take all necessary steps to promote the standard of Higher Secondary Education.

Committees

To carry out its functions, the Council with the approval of the State Government constitutes committees, such as Recognition

Committee, Syllabus Committee, Examination Committee, Finance Committee, and Appeal Committee. It is the duty of the Council to advise the State Government on all matters relating to the Higher Secondary Education.

Decentralisation

Keeping in view the above stated functions, and large number of students, the Council has decentralised its activities. Jurisdiction of Council extends to 18 districts in WB. There is one head office (Vidyasagar Bhavan) and four regional offices (Kolkata, Bardwan, North Bengal, Murshidabad) that cater to the needs of students residing in these areas. In each of the four regions, one Deputy Secretary and one Assistant Secretary are placed.

Composition of Council

The Council consists of the following members:

(a) The President (appointed by the State Government);

Ex-officio Members:

(b) The President of the West Bengal Board of Secondary Education;
(c) The Director of School Education;
(d) The Director of Technical Education;
(e) The Director of Industries
(f) The Director of Agriculture;
(g) The Director, SCERT;

Nominated Members:

(h) One women interested in the field of education;
(i) One principal of a college imparting instructions in Higher Secondary Education;
(j) One Dean of any faculty of Bidhan Chandra Krishi Vidaylaya
(k) One head of a Higher Secondary Education.

Elected Members:

(l) One person from the employees of the Council, and
(m) Six teachers of secondary schools elected as per provisions of the Council.

Representative Members:

(n) Two representatives from the West Bengal Legislative Assembly,

(o) One person each of the Court of Vidyasagar Univeristy of Midnapore, Jadavpur, University of Rabindra Bharati, University of Kalyani, University of Calcutta, University of Burdwan, and the North Bengal University.

Education System Imparted by the Council

At the Senior Secondary level, there are three Boards: West Bengal Council for Higher Secondary Education, Higher Secondary Madrasah and Rabindra Mukta Vidyalaya (RMV). In terms of the Act, at the Senior Secondary level West Bengal Council for Higher Secondary Education is responsible for designing and prescribing curricula and syllabi. Higher Secondary Madrasahs and RMV at higher secondary level follow the same curricula as prescribed by the West Bengal Council of Higher Secondary Education.

There are three types of schools in the State for Higher Secondary Education. The first type is Integrated Higher Secondary School (Classes with I to XII), their total number at present being 2797. The second type is that of Independent Schools, which at present are only 18, running only two classes, i.e., XI and XII. The third category is of those higher secondary schools, which are attached with colleges, in which duration of course is of one year. At present there are 141 colleges in which higher secondary classes are conducted. In these institutions, about 4 lakh students are studying. Bhabatosh Dutta, Dr. Ashok Mitra and Kothari Commission all have disapproved having higher secondary courses in colleges. According to them, in schools it is a two-year course, while in colleges it is of one-year duration. The conditions of teaching in schools and colleges are totally different. This ambiguity affected the planning of syllabus and examination. It was difficult to cover two years syllabus in one year; this is excessively heavy. To cover the syllabus, teachers give little home work or assignments. Therefore, content of the syllabus does not really prepare the children for the intensive higher secondary course. Now the State Government is withdrawing such sections from colleges in a phased manner. The higher secondary schools have two streams: (1) General Stream, (2) Vocational Stream. Directorate of School Education is the controlling authority for schools.

General Stream

General stream contains three types of courses, i.e., Arts, Science and Commerce.

Vocational Stream

Kothari Commission gave greater emphasis to the vocational education, and recommended to include various vocational subjects in the higher secondary education curriculum in order to help those students who leave education at this stage to earn their living. This inclusion of quite a large number of subjects will also help students who continue their education further. The Commission also aspired to increase enrolment up to 50 per cent in vocational courses. The Ashok Mitra Commission too recommended for a wide range of vocational courses. Considering the drop-out rate, these Commissions strongly proposed to enrich and enhance the grip of vocational courses in the higher secondary courses. The West Bengal Council of Higher Secondary Education has adopted the recommendations of Kothari Commission keeping its central idea intact. At the terminal point of Class VIII, opportunity for vocational education is provided in the Industrial Training Institutes. After Class X, the scope for vocational training has been created in the Polytechnics, and after Class XII, students can at least theoretically go for a degree level technical education in engineering and allied areas, and medical education etc.

There are many limitations in the vocational courses and as such these courses have met a very low level of response from the students. The Board has faced some grave practical problems; some of them are:

(a) Students, who opt for the Vocational Education Courses at Higher Secondary level, generally monopolise admission to the Polytechnics. This leaves little option for the students who want to pursue vocational stream at the level of XII.

(b) At the Higher Secondary level, not even one per cent of the students opt for the vocational stream. It is considered that the content of the course hardly gives them professional excellence.

(c) Completion of the vocational course at the Higher Secondary level does not ensure one to get straight admission in colleges to pursue Bachelors Degree. Therefore, currently the Council has consolidated its position on vocational education and

> has been constantly working on the syllabus and curriculum. Courses in Medical, Engineering, Agriculture and Pharmacy have been introduced. In order to stretch the scope of vocational education and to meet the need of students to make their studies job-oriented, special emphasis is being given on these aspects and for this purpose the Council has been collaborating with the Board of Secondary Education, Maharashtra. The Council has conducted field studies to improve the scope of vocational education, and has introduced vocational education in 53 higher secondary schools, which offer various courses.

Nevertheless, the State proudly claims to have alternative vocational courses in several Polytechnics. Some of the institutes of good repute fetch high number of students (for example, College of Leather Technology, Institute of Printing Technology). The absorption capacity of such institutes is very low and percentage may range from 4.8 to 10. The Ashok Mitra Commission proposed not only to enhance the quality of the curriculum but also the linking it up with the host of opportunities in the labour market.

In spite of the State's claim, the position of vocational education is very grim. Table 5.9 shows that the enrolment in the vocational courses is not only alarmingly poor, but is also steadily declining. During 1998, the students at vocational courses were 0.72 per cent. The number slightly increased in 1999. But after that, in subsequent years, the enrolment has again declined.

Table 5.9: Enrolment in Vocational Stream under the West Bengal Council of Higher Secondary Education

Year	*Total Enrolment (General and Vocational)*	*Enrolment in Vocational*	*Percent of col. 3 to col. 2*
1998	374136	2696	0.72
1999	356190	3110	0.87
2000	369971	2805	0.76
2001	384466	2681	0.70
2002	386408	2469	0.64

Source: WBCHS

Examination Practice

Examinations of the Board are held in the month of March. Practice of reappearing in exam does not exist. The total course contents of Classes XI and XII are covered in the exam. After the result, merit list is prepared. During 2002-03, over 50 students secured more than 90 per cent marks and 13 students scored 200 out of 200 marks.

To avoid malpractice in examination, special codes are given to roll number issued to students. Student's identification is known through roll number and registration number. The roll number is always of 10 digits. First three digits point to district code, next three digits point to institute's code, next two digits show the stream, i.e., General or Vocational, and the last two digits indicate the gender of the student, i.e., boy or girl. Every year, district codes are changed to maintain the secrecy or identity of students.

To facilitate the examination process, the Council has decentralised its activities. There are 4 regional offices, which cater to the needs of students residing in those areas. These are at Kolkata, Burdwan, Murshidabad, and North Bengal.

Examination Result

The analysis of results was done to see the performance of schools. The results classification is done on the basis of vocational and general stream, which is further classified according to the regular, continuing and special education.

Table 5.10 indicates that pass percentage for both male and female students has increased from 2000 to 2001. In continuing education, pass percentage is very low in comparison with that of the regulars and the special education category. Table 5.11 shows that the number of students enrolling in the vocational stream is very low in comparison to that in general stream; the presence of female students is extremely dismal. It seems that vocational education is generally considered suitable for male students and parents' preference goes in favour of general education for the female students.

Table 5.10: Result of General Candidates in 2000 and 2001

General Stream	*2000*				*2001*			
Enrolled	*Regular*	*Continuing Education*	*Special Education*	*Total*	*Regular*	*Continuing Education*	*Special Education*	*Total*
Male	154213	18486	48486	221185	162756	17881	46159	226796
Female	99441	7563	33812	140816	106930	7784	35867	15081
Total	253654	26049	82298	362001	269686	25665	82026	377377
Appeared								
Male	152044	13176	48468	213688	160394	12844	46159	219397
Female	98614	5554	33812	137980	106003	5724	35867	147594
Total	250658	18730	82280	351668	266397	18568	82026	366991
Passed								
Male %	65.95	26.47	48.06	59.36	67.07	25.85	48.11	60.53
Female%	61.76	18.04	46.12	56.11	65.50	20.38	51.36	60.18
1st Div								
Male	19279	168	23	19470	18390	135	41	18566
Female	13091	43	26	13160	13707	46	64	13817
Total	32370	211	49	32630	32097	181	105	32383
2nd Div								
Male	45846	1104	3011	49961	49980	1145	3773	54898
Female	30747	302	2777	33826	35663	348	4229	40240
Total	76593	1406	5788	83787	85643	1493	8002	95138
Pass Div								
Male	34986	2203	20228	57417	38968	2018	18359	59345
Female	17011	654	12776	30441	19883	770	14115	34768
Total	51997	2857	33004	87858	58851	2788	32474	94113

Source: Annual Report, WBBSE, 2002.

Table 5.11: Result of Vocational Stream Candidates in 2000 and 2001

Vocational Stream	*2000*				*2001*			
	Regular	*Continuing*	*Special*	*Total*	*Regular*	*Continuing*	*Special*	*Total*
Enrolled								
Male	1467	414	575	2456	1541	374	417	2332
Female	235	42	72	349	250	48	51	349
Total	1702	456	647	2805	1791	422	468	2681
Appeared								
Male	1448	317	575	2340	1528	291	417	2236
Female	234	37	72	343	249	39	51	339
Total	1682	354	647	2683	1777	330	468	2575
Passed								
Male, %	61.6	16.77	52.61	55.67	61.19	15	45.08	51.65
Female, %	61.11	16.22	58.33	55.68	51.41	23.08	50.98	48.08
1st Div								
Male	568	15	72	655	596	7	50	653
Female	83	0	12	95	81	5	9	95
Total	651	15	84	750	677	12	59	748
2nd Div								
Male	307	38	217	562	321	21	129	471
Female	52	6	28	86	46	4	14	64
Total	359	44	245	648	367	25	143	535
3rd Div								
Male	17	0	13	30	18	4	9	31
Female	8	0	2	10	1	Nil	3	4
Total	25	0	15	40	19	4	12	35

Source: Annual Report, WBBSE, 2002.

The President Prof Jotirmay Mukhopadhyay and other officials of the West Bengal Council of Higher Secondary Education were interviewed to know the status of Council and the changes that have been incorporated from time to time in the Council. The interview was conducted through structured questionnaire covering three issues: Curriculum, Instructional process, and Examination reform.

Changes in the System

A. Curriculum

(a) Preparation of the manual of textbooks

The Council frames the curriculum and syllabus. It publishes only language books; books on other subjects are published by private publishers. For this purpose, proper guidelines are given to them regarding number of chapters, and the number of pages the book will contain. If any body fails to follow the norms, his license is cancelled. In case of publishing textbooks for the secondary and higher secondary levels, many publishing houses are in the habit of violating the rules and norms prescribed by the Board and the Council. In many cases, bulkiness of the books becomes the cause of panic for the students. Thus the prescribed syllabi are artificially and unnecessarily made to appear much heavier than they actually are. Further, variations in information and data presentation in different books create confusion among the students. Therefore, the problem has been solved by preparing the manual of all the textbooks.

(b) Curriculum updation

After a long gap of 15 years, the curriculum has been updated recently. Care was taken on three aspects while updating the curriculum, i.e., comparability of standards with X class, continuity (all India coverage), and easy to adapt for students. On the basis of new curriculum, the Council is planning to develop teaching modules. The President feels that if teaching modules are prepared, it may help to stop the flourishing tuition practice.

(c) Curriculum at par with NCERT guidelines

The Council revised all subject components of the textbooks for the year 2004-05. They have improved the syllabi of English and Bengali. In English, along with Shakespeare, Elizabethian Period of 19th and 20th century, Indian contribution to the English literature has also been added. It is kept in view that the syllabi of all the subjects should contain quality and be at par with other states and comply with the NCERT guidelines too. The President felt unhappy on the attendance level being low at senior secondary level and that its main cause was a lot of stress being placed on private tuitions.

(d) Composite curriculum at senior secondary level

In West Bengal, the examinations are given on the basis of composite units taught in Classes XI and XII (for H.S.). While in other states, in most of the cases, the final examinations cover the topics meant for Class XII only.

(e) New vocational courses introduced

West Bengal has been the first state to introduce vocational education in the country. Recently, many new vocational courses were introduced at the senior secondary level, covering Agriculture, Trade and Commerce, and Technical, Electrical and Mechanical subjects. The students of these courses get admission to Polytechnics in the second year. This year, the West Bengal Council of Higher Secondary Education reviewed the subject's pattern and introduced 'Information Technology' as one of the elective subjects.

(f) Publication of journal

The Council publishes a monthly journal *Shiksha Darpan*. The journal is very popular with teachers and students alike as it contains various teaching-learning materials and Council's circulars. It is an effective bridge as it links remote areas of the schools with the Council headquarters.

B. Instructional Process

(a) Capacity building of teachers

For academic up-liftment and also to improve the instructional process, the Council organises seminars, and teacher's orientation programmes. It was mentioned that the Council is planning to train 40,000 teachers, and for that purpose, teaching material is ready.

(b) Coverage in rural/urban and remote areas

The Council is working in such a way that more and more students from rural and remote areas may join the schools. The Council believes that the government schools are equally good and that there were 18 schools that have found a place in the merit list of Council Board exam with 0 per cent failure during 2003-04, and that 17 of them were government schools. This has boosted the status of government schools and contributed significantly in the students' strength in these schools.

C. Evaluation Process

(a) Computerisation of results

The results of the Council exams have been computerised since 1991. The Council claims that it has created precedence in India by issuing Marksheets and Certificates on the very day of the declaration of the results.

(b) Assessment of answer scripts

Practical answer scripts of both the general stream and the vocational stream are assessed by the examiners appointed for practical examination, but such scripts are finally assessed by the concerned Head Examiners to confirm the marks given.

(c) Decentralisation

For facilitation of evaluation process, the Council has decentralised its evaluation activities by dividing West Bengal into four regions, i.e., Kolkata, Burdwan, Murshidabad and North Bengal.

(d) Evaluation process made transparent

The examinee student's identification is known through his roll number and registration number issued by the Council. The examination being transparent, the question paper leaking has never happened. To make it more transparent, the Council has introduced post-public review (PPR) along with post-publication scrutiny (PPS). If at the time of re-evaluation of answer scripts, any discrepancy is found, the Council has to pay back Rs. 2000 to the student.

(e) Honor to meritorious students

If a candidate obtains 80 per cent marks in a subject, he/she is awarded a commendation 'Letter' in the subject and the award is indicated in the mark-sheet. If a candidate obtains 75 per cent marks in the aggregate, he/she is declared to have passed with 'Star' which is indicated in the mark-sheet.

If a candidate, other than a candidate of special category of the general stream courses, does not appear or fails to obtain the minimum pass marks in any one compulsory elective subject and if he/she offers an optional elective subject at the said examination and secures pass marks in that subject, he/she is given the benefit of the marks obtained in the same elective subject by inter-changing the relevant compulsory elective subject for passing the examination; provided that if a candidate does not intend, for any reason whatsoever, to pass the examination under the condition prescribed above, he/she shall have to intimate the Council accordingly in writing through his/her institution within thirty days from the date of receipt of the mark-sheet and also has to surrender the mark-sheet for necessary correction.

If a candidate fails to pass in one compulsory subject by not more than 5 per cent marks, he/she shall be given credit by transfer of marks from the highest marks scored by him or her in a compulsory subject to make up the deficiency in the subject in which he/she fails.

(f) Publish the list of meritorious students

The Council publishes a list of meritorious students, but the Council president feels that this practice should be abandoned or discontinued, as 'Science' students cannot be compared with 'Arts' students.

(g) Website of the Council

The Council has its own website. Details about its Act, rules, regulations are displayed. It also supports the results of the senior secondary examination.

(h) Legal issues

When a student is caught copying in an examination hall from printed material by the invigilator, or when he is found to be a dummy candidate in place of the right candidate, it becomes a legal issue, which is tackled by the Examination Committee. But generally, these types of cases are very few.

(i) Examinations transparency

The president of the Council mentioned very confidently that the Council examinations are always transparent. Leaking of question papers never happens.

(j) Independent schools

The Council officials, mentioned that independent schools are privately managed; therefore, it is very difficult to supervise them. The president feels that Managing Committees of the independent schools should have Council nominees on their boards. There is a difference in the curricular load of the examination. In most cases, the final examinations are held covering the topics meant for Class X (for secondary) and Class XII (for H.S.). However, in West Bengal, the examinations are conducted on the basis of composite units taught in Classes IX and X (for secondary) and XI and XII (for H.S.).

Recommendations

- Multi-disciplinary subjects had not been introduced yet. All the subjects are traditional in nature.
- The idea of 'school cluster', if properly structured and put into action may be of immense value in making up some of the deficiencies of the system and thereby elevating quality of teaching. Such clusters can play a positive role in mobilising and sharing resources, coordinating academic and extra-academic programmes, decentralising examination and arranging important events related to social service and activity-based learning.
- The new pattern of school education as formulated by the Kothari Commission was introduced in West Bengal in 1976 with one significant deviation. Higher Secondary course has been taught in both schools and colleges. In schools it is of two years, while in colleges it is of one year. The conditions of teaching in schools and colleges are totally different. This ambiguity affected the planning of syllabus and examination. It was difficult to cover two years syllabus in one year. The syllabi refer to be excessively heavy. To cover the syllabus, teachers give little homework or assignments. Therefore, content of the syllabus does not really prepare the children to bear more intensive burden of the higher secondary course. Therefore, higher secondary courses of colleges need to be phased out as soon as possible.
- There is no research unit in the Council. Academic unit generally looks after framing of curricula, up-gradation of schools, introduction of new subjects, publication of books, and organising seminars and orientation programmes for teachers.

A research unit would help the Council on future actions and directions to be taken for overall quality improvement in academic and management functions, and the examination wings of the Council can also be prioritised for action.

- There is a need to develop external linkages and networking with the Directorate of Education, SCERT, universities, NCERT and NIEPA. The purpose of the linkages is to seek co-operation in capacity building programmes, to know the latest trends in education, and to share results of researches etc.
- Need of computer assisted teaching to all the teachers.

West Bengal Board of Madrasah Education

Introduction

Madrasah is an Arabic word, meaning educational institution/school imparting education to all, irrespective of religion, caste and gender. During the long period of Muslim rule in India a network of thousands of educational institutions had been built up across the country. These institutions were generally known as madrasahs. It included Maktabs, Madrasahs and Jamias. Maktabs were lowest step of the education system then in operation and were meant for an elementary Islamic education. These were mostly attached with the mosques but many of them were run in private houses also. Earlier, financial donations were given to Madrasahs by local Muslim population, but in course of its development, the state government has patronised the Madrasah Education with financial and academic support.

History of the Board

Pre-Independence

In West Bengal, the Madrasah system of education has a very rich history and is one of the oldest education systems in India. It came to India from Sindh with Arabs and spread to other parts of India. The Madrasah system of education had a turning point with the conquest of India by the then East India Company. In 1781 Mugal Emperor Shah Alam II handed over Diwani (Revenue and Civil Justice) of Bengal to East India Company. The East India Company needed trained officers for running the revenue administration and judiciary of Bengal. As a result, Calcutta Madrasah was established by Warren Hastings, the first Governor General of the East India Company. Later when in 1857, the Calcutta University was established for the development of English system of education, Calcutta Madrasah was left under the jurisdiction of Calcutta University, and because of political, educational and financial reasons, Madrasah education was continued. In 1915, the Madrasah Education system had a new turn. On the recommendations of Mahammadan Education Advisory Committee in 1915, some subjects of general education were introduced in Madrasahs. That pattern has continued since then. The Madrasahs where these subjects were introduced are known as the New Scheme of Madrasah or High Madrasah Education System. At the same time, some Madrasahs continued under the earlier pattern of education known as Senior Madrasahs. Different Boards were entrusted the conduct of the new High Madrasah and Senior Madrasah examinations. The Board of Islamic Intermediate and University of Dacca used to conduct the High Madrasah examinations and the Board of Central Madrasah was established in 1927 for conducting three types of examinations namely, Junior (Alim), Senior (Fazil) and Title (Mumtazul Muhammadin) respectively after six, eight and ten years of study. The same situation continued till 1947 when India was partitioned and attained Independence.

After Independence

After partition, the main Board was shifted to Dacca and an interim Board named West Bengal Madrasah Education Board was set up in Hoogly. The Principal of the Islamic College was nominated as the Ex-officio Registrar of the Board. Calcutta Madrasah was also re-opened in 1949 at the initiative of Maulana Abul Kalam Azad, the then Education Minister of Government of India. The Madrasah Board was then transferred to Calcutta Madrasah. In 1964, the Board was renamed as West Bengal Board of Madrasah Education (WBBME). In 1973 the Board was reconstituted having 15 members with president, and an advisory body.

Status and Jurisdiction of the Board

In 1994, the WBBME was given an autonomous status like the School Education Board/Council in West Bengal. Since then, the Board has powers to direct, supervise and control both types of Madrasah (Junior and High Madrasahs) education in the state. It functions on the guidelines suggested by the Government through the Madrasah Education Department of the State Government. Recommendations duly approved by the State Government are acted upon.

Organisational Structure

To strengthen and decentralise the Madrasah education, the Government appointed a President and Secretary as permanent members of the Board.

In addition, the Board has an Advisory Body consisting of the President of WBBME, WBBSE, WBCHSE and the President of the West Bengal Primary Education, the Director of School Education, and the Head of the Department of Arabic, Calcutta University. The Principal of Calcutta Madrasah is *ex-officio* member. Amongst the nominated members are: two heads of the recognised Madrasahs (one high Madrasah and one Senior Madrasah), two members of the West Bengal Legislative Assembly, one person who is imparting instruction in Arabic or Persian language and is a whole time member of teaching staff, one expert in Islamic Culture and theology, one woman interested in Madrasah education. Among thirteen elected members ten are whole time permanent members of the teaching staff of recognised Madrasah, two persons from the whole time and permanent members from non-teaching staff of the recognised Madrasah, one whole time permanent staff of the Board.

Major Functions of the Board

The function of the Board is to hold public examinations of High Madrasahs and Senior Madrasahs (Alim, Fazil, Kamil and Mumtazul Muhammadin). In addition it holds Test Examination of External candidates preparatory to High Madrasah. It gives recognition to Junior Madrasahs (V-VIII), High Madrasahs (IX-X) and Senior Madrasahs (I-X). Also it conducts in-service orientation programmes for teachers and heads of Madrasahs.

Committees

To perform the above functions following Committees are constitutes:

- Recognition Committee
- Syllabus Committee
- Examination Committee
- Finance Committee
- Appeal Committee
- Committee constituted under Section 18 of the Act.

Education System

West Bengal Board of Madrasah Education offers two types of Madrasah education systems: 1) High Madrasah Education System, 2) Senior Madrasah Education System.

Courses and Programmes

The curriculum and syllabus of High Madrasah is identical to those of W.B. Board of Secondary Education except History, Geography and Advance Arabic. Additional Islamic History is same as those prescribed by West Bengal Board of Secondary Education. The History syllabus excludes the period of Indian History prior to Mughals and includes Islamic History (from advent of Islam up to the period of fourth Caliph Hazard Ali (R). The syllabus of Geography excludes some topics from Regional Economic and Human Geography part prescribed by the West Bengal Board of Secondary Education. In addition Arabic language is compulsory additional subject in High Madrasahs. The High Madrasah Examination after the end of Class X has been made equivalent to the Madhyamik Examination of the W.B. Board of Secondary Education.

Senior Madrasah has four stages: (1) Alim stage includes ten classes and the subjects are Arabic, Hadith, Tafir, Figh and Faraid. In order to forge a closer affinity with the Madhyaymik Pariksha, a number of basic subjects such as Mathematics, Physical Science, Life Science, History, Geography, with mother tongue, i.e., Bengali or Urdu and English are also added. The external examination has also been declared as equivalent to the Madhyamik Pariksha and the students of this stage are thus eligible for admission to Higher Secondary courses in and outside of the state. (2) Next is the Fazil stage having 2 years duration, dominantly having Arabic language, will theological contents of study. Fazil is not recognised by the Higher Secondary Council as equivalent to Higher Secondary. But those candidates, who passed Fazil Examination with English as an additional subject, were considered eligible for admission to the pre-university (Arts) course of the University of Calcutta. Subsequently, the WBCHSE allowed such students to be admitted to Class XI in a higher secondary school. (3) The third stage is known as Kamil and is not recognised by any University since the course is dominantly theology-oriented. (4) The last and the highest stage is known as Mumtazul Muhammadin, popularly known as the P.G. course; it is also not recognised by any university. The course content is absolutely theological.

Expansion of Madrasah Education

In course of its development, the state government has patronised the Madrasah Education with financial and academic support. There has been steady increase in the number of these institutions, students and teachers.

The state government is willing to extend the benefit of education to all the population in the state including the education of minorities and SC/STs. With this idea there has been a steady increase in the number of Madrasahs as well as in the student population in Madrasahs. Table 5.12 indicates that the total number of High and Senior Madrasahs increased from 9 to 508 from the period 1948-49 to 2004-05. The growth of Madrasahs was not alike over the years. Up to 2001-02 many new Madrasahs were opened. In case of High Madrasahs they increased from 7 to 405 from 1948-49 to 2004-05. In the same way Senior Madrasahs grew from 2 to 103 from 1948-49 to 1991-92, then remained static up to 2004-05.

Table 5.13 shows that the number of students is more in High Madrasahs than in Senior Madrasahs. This indicates students' inclination toward traditional secondary education than opting theological subjects that have poor employability. During 1998-99, there were 13786 students in High Madrasahs in comparison to 1575 in Senior Madrasahs. The number of students increased to 16171 in High Madrasahs and 2665 in Senior Madrasahs from 1998-99 to 2002-03.

Table 5.12: Distribution of number of Madrasahs in West Bengal

Year	*High Madrasahs*	*Senior Madrasahs*	*Total*
1948-49	7	2	9
1977-78	92	74	166
1991-92	174	103	277
1998-99	215	103	318
1999-00	220	103	323
2000-01	234	103	337
2001-02	238	103	341
2002-03	238	103	341
2003-04	N.A.	103	N.A.
2004-05	405	103	508

Table 5.13: Distribution of Enrolment in the Madrasahs

Year	High Madrasahs	Senior Madrasahs
1998-99	13786	1575
1999-00	14122	1771
2000-01	15428	1864
2001-02	16034	2242
2002-03	16171	2665

Examination System

WBBME conducts examination of High Madrasahs and Senior Madrasahs (Alim, Fazil, Kamil and Mumtazul Muhammadin). Table 5.14 shows that in High Madrasahs pass percentage of students is continuously increasing. During 1997-98, the pass percentage at High Madrasahs was 50 per cent, which increased to 64 per cent in the next five years, i.e., in 2002-03. In Senior Madrasahs, at Alim stage, pass percentage varies from 61 per cent to 67 per cent. At Fazil stage, it varies from 61 to 79, at Kamil stage it varies from 68 to 83 per cent, and at MM stage, the variation is quite high; in 1998-99 pass percentage was 100, in 2000-01 it reduced to only 61 per cent; again it is showing a rising trend.

Though the successful students in the Senior Madrasah examinations have no direct opportunity to go for higher studies in the general stream of education and their employment opportunities too are restricted, even then the pass percentage of students are increasing over the years. In all the stages, i.e., from Alim to MM the pass percentage has been increasing at a higher rate in these courses than in High Madrasahs.

Table 5.14: Examination Results

Year	Appeared in Types of Examinations					% of pass				
	High Madrasahs	Alim	Fazil	Kamil	MM	High Madrasahs	Alim	Fazil	Kamil	MM
1997	12,816	938	235	–	–	50.42	61.00	65.30	–	–
1998	12,879	1022	273	130	19	55.15	64.97	65.20	80.76	100.00
1999	13,174	1,169	305	111	54	62.00	63.00	61.00	68.00	76.00
2000	14,239	1,218	342	190	98	57.46	62.80	68.42	68.42	61.22
2001	15,166	1,545	337	198	50	63.25	67.96	79.52	73.23	88.00
2002	15696	1835	315	268	116	64.15	65.61	75.23	83.96	84.48

Interaction with Board Officials

A structured interview schedule was carried out to know the perceptions of the President, Dr. Abdus Sattar, of the W.B. Board of Madrasah Education, and Shri O.A. Rehman, Secretary, W.B. Board of Madrasah Education and Md. Refatullah, Consultant (Ex-Director, SCERT) regarding the role of the Board in improving the quality of secondary education and change needed to achieve quality. Talking on the reforms and innovations, Dr. Sattar mentioned about the following reforms that were implemented in Madrasah education system as recommended from time to time by various committees:

Reforms and Changes in the Madrasah Education System Over the Years

- The state government believes in decentralisation as the means to success for education. Therefore, its policy is to expand the level of decentralisation in every sphere, including Madrasah education. In this respect, government took a historic step to give Madrasah Board an autonomous status in 1994 like that given to School Education Board.
- The Board introduced re-oriented syllabus and curriculum as prescribed by WBBSE and WBCHSE from 1981 onwards, thus establishing parity with WBBSE and WBCHSE.
- The re-oriented curriculum tried to accommodate some essential subjects of studies from general education at each level from Class I to Class X. The syllabi of these subjects from Classes I to V were taken from Primary Board and for Classes VI to X from WBBSE with certain modifications to make education of Alim stage at par with secondary pattern of education. The syllabi of additional subjects, viz. English, Bengali, Urdu and Persian of Fazil stage were taken from WBCHSE. In the process, a few subjects from theology group had to be eliminated and volume of contents of some remaining subjects reduced at the Alim stage.
- The uncovered portion of religious subjects was accommodated in the curriculum of Fazil by increasing the duration of the course of studies from two years to four years (Fazil two years and Kamil two years) for 'those who have special aptitude for studying classical Arabic and Persian literature, and those who strive for having wide knowledge about different aspects of Islamic religion and culture, those

who aspire for religious education to be an end in itself, and those who think it unwise to judge the value and utility of this type of education from the standpoints of employment opportunities in future life.'

- The Board is planning to start vocational and skill-oriented courses in collaboration with the technical education department to help students in the field of engineering, and medicine. For that reason, Board is planning to conduct seminar in collaboration with Netaji Open University and West Bengal University of Technical Education.
- For improving quality education, the Board introduced Achievement Level Tests (ALTs) in High and Senior High Madrasahs in collaboration with the Guidance Foundation, Kolkata.
- Continuous and Comprehensive Evaluation is introduced in all types of Madrasah schools in order to raise achievement level of students.
- Before the commencement of Board examination, meeting with president, and heads of school is held to support schools for any type of help or guidance.
- For improving internal quality, a detailed Board circular embodying annual calendar, rules of the managing committee, heads of the Madrasahs, teachers and all concerned, examination evaluation schedules and organising of co-curricular activities, morning assembly, value education etc. has been prepared and sent to all the heads for implementing and pursuing the activities as directed.
- Board publishes a detailed examination calendar concerning external Madrasah Examination every year, so that these examinations could be conducted smoothly and efficiently through the involvement of all on time bound programmes.
- The Board has started printing photos of the regular and external candidates on the Registration Certificates and Admit Cards for identification at the different examinations of the Board since 2003.
- In order that religion should not play a negative effect on the academic achievement of candidates in the external examinations at different levels, the Board unanimously decided to write off the names of the candidates on the answer scripts. Rather it has directed the Madrasahs to train the

teachers and the students to be accustomed the Registration number and the roll number on the answer-scripts for identification.

- The explosion of knowledge, communication and technology has casted shadow on every walk of life, including education. True to the tune of the age, the state government has introduced Computer Literacy Programme in 18 High Madrasahs. The Board of Madrasah Education, accordingly, has introduced Computer Application as an additional subject in the High Madrasah Examination since 2001. In addition, stress is laid on Computer aided learning and frequently orientation programmes are organised for the teachers. The Board has already issued circulars to the Heads of all High Madrasahs to introduce computer literacy education from Class VII to Class XII. Also the scope of Information Technology is further extended in collaboration with the Jadavpur University by which computer education will be imparted to girls in High Madrasah. Needless to say that the process of computer education in Madrasah may be termed as a revolution and it may go to create a modern atmosphere in the organisation.
- The Board feels that collaboration with RMV has a bigger role to play for the education of the dropouts after Class VII and economically and socially backward children and adults under the innovative scheme of the RMV. These Madrasah centres are likewise open to all irrespective of religion, caste, creed and gender.
- In order to provide variety, better options and to meet demands of the students and guardians, the Board has increased the number of additional subjects in the High Madrasah curriculum. In place of 10 subjects, 20 subjects have been included as additional subjects.
- The Board has been accepted and recognised by the NCERT as its participating mailing partner.
- Collaborative programmes aim at quality enhancement by sharing experience and getting training in quality areas. This Board has over the years, undertaken collaborative programmes for academic improvement with SCERT, W.B. State Council of Elementary Education (SSA and DPEP) and the national agencies like NCERT and NIEPA.

- Salaries and service conditions of Heads of schools of Madrasahs, and teaching and non-teaching staff of Senior Madrasah, were brought at par with the higher secondary schools. Earlier Senior Madrasahs did not have any equivalence with the state's general education system. They were privately managed and service conditions of teachers were very insecure and financially weak. Committees were set up from time to time by the state government to review the status of teachers. In accordance with the recommendations of the committees, the state government introduced for the first time in 1980 a standard pay scale for the teaching and non-teaching staff of Senior Madrasahs.
- A journal *Madrasah Darpan* is published regularly on a quarterly basis from 2001. Each issue contains articles on various issues of educational improvement and evaluation of secondary course, which are helpful to Madrasah students. In addition, it also contains Board's activities in detail, notifications, and directives to its recognised institutions. The journal acts as a link between the Board and the Madrasahs.
- The Board knows well that without having good quality books they cannot infuse quality values in the system. The Board is in the process of preparing such good quality textbooks in all subjects and for all classes from VI-X except those published by the WBBSE The Board will start producing the textbooks full fledged by 2004-2005. Currently, the Board of Madrasah Education was procuring textbooks in English and Arithmetic from Board of Secondary Education. Books on other subjects are published in the same manner as other Boards are publishing.
- The notion of Madrasah Complex has been concieved with the aim of harmonising the learning process, material and the streams as well as effecting a balanced development of the learner's consciousness as much as possible. All the Madrasahs, except a few, lack the infrastructural facilities and this Madrasah complex can lead to quality improvement and management of academic and non-academic activities.
- Apart from its educational enrichment and school improvement programmes, the Board is deeply engaged with the UNICEF for undertaking social service and educational programmes in the state, particularly for the upliftment of

the minority and backward communities. These include social, mental and physical health and other common awareness programmes, like polio eradication, routine immunisation, etc. No other Board has come forward in such programmes.

Rabindra Mukta Vidhalaya (State Open School), Kolkata

National Scenario

During last century, especially in 60s, all the developing countries were facing problems in the field of education because of two reasons: (i) the increasing demand for education, and (ii) to meet the demand governments of developing countries had resource crunch. Many studies were conducted to overcome the problem. Coombs, in his study, mentioned that 'World Education Crisis' would continue and might aggravate because the states, particularly those in Asia, would find it increasingly difficult to allocate necessary funds for this purpose. Therefore, during this period need was felt to adopt less expensive modes of delivery for education. As a result, non-formal education came into existence as an alternative system, of which open learning is a major component. The open schooling system offers opportunities for part-time study to those sections of adult population that for some reason or the other have not been able to complete school education and are not in a position to join the formal system. 'The objective of National Open Schooling was to provide a parallel system of non-formal schooling, aimed at working adults, disadvantaged groups, and other out-of-school learners' (Sujatha 2002).

In this context, India has made rapid progress. First, distance education institutions were set up in order to provide secondary education through correspondence. Later in 1989, based on the framework of the National Policy on Education (1986), National Open School was set up as an autonomous institution. In addition some states also established state-level Open Schools. According to Mukhopadhyay and Parhar (1997) "With one National Open School and eleven state-open schools, India has the single largest distance education system in the world, both in terms of number of institutions and enrolment at the secondary level." In 1990, the Government of India authorised the National Open School to conduct examinations and to act as the certifying authority at the secondary and senior secondary levels.

'Open Schooling as an alternate system designs its own programmes and frames its rules and procedures keeping in mind the special needs and problems of its target groups. The regulations are, so to say, tailor-made to meet the learner's requirements instead of facing the learners to submit to their rigidity' (Report School Education Committee, West Bengal 2002).

The Government of West Bengal established the State Open School in 1997 as an autonomous Board and as a wing of School Education Directorate. In 2001, Rabindra Mukta Vidhyalaya (RMV) bill was placed in Legislative Assembly and has since been accepted and passed and made into an Act. The RMV Act entrusts the Vidhyalya with the task of imparting open education at the secondary and senior secondary levels through distance learning mode, supported by study centres. RMV's statutory role also includes offering courses in vocational areas. Subsequently a mechanism for examination and certification was established in RMV.

Thus State Open School was reshaped and renamed as 'Rabindra Mukta Vidhyalaya' (RMV), with a view to provide modern, flexible, life oriented education at the secondary level to the school dropouts after Class VIII, to take quality education to the doorstep of those who are deprived of school education in rural areas, the urban poor, SC/ST and other disadvantaged groups. More flexible and less rigid rules and procedures have been formulated taking into account their special needs and circumstances.

(i) Organisational Structure of the Board

The Board consists of the Chairman, Director, Heads of the Academic Departments, Secretary, and Tutors.

(ii) Courses and Programmes Offered

RMV serves both the secondary school as well as the senior secondary school children. Regarding choice of subjects, RMV offers full autonomy to the learners.

Secondary Level

At the secondary level, RMV offers at present eleven subjects: Bengali, English, Mathematics, Physical Science, Life Science, History, Geography, Political Science, Economics, Home Science, and Commerce.

Senior Secondary Level

At the senior secondary level, RMV offers ten subjects: Bengali, English, History, Commercial Geography, Political Science, Education, Economics, Mathematics, Accountancy, Business Organisation and Management.

(iii) Main Functions of the Board

Main functions of the Board are preparation of the study materials, recognition of study centres, and conduct of examinations, issuing of certificates to successful candidates and counseling to students through the study centres.

Secondary Certificate Courses

Admissions are very flexible. At the secondary level any one who has completed 14 years of age and has acquired education up to class VIII standard, either formally or by self-learning, can seek admission. There is no age limit. The course offers a choice of two languages and nine other subjects. Minimum of five subjects, including one language either Bengali or English, is compulsory. However, a student is free to choose as many subjects as he/she desires to learn, may be one or all the subjects. But if a student desires equivalence he/she has to clear all the stipulated compulsory subjects by the WBBSE.

Senior Secondary Certificate Courses

At the senior secondary level, students who have passed secondary examination from West Bengal Board of Secondary Education or its equivalent examination, including Rabindra Mukta Vidayalya, are eligible for admission to any study centre recognised by Rabindra Mukta Vidhyalaya. Like Secondary certificate courses, a student is free to offer any number of subjects according to his/her choice, but if a student desires equivalence, he/she will have to clear the compulsory and minimum number of elective subjects as stipulated for the senior secondary examination under WBCHSE. It means passing with two language subjects and three optional subjects, then only a student becomes eligible for the issue of Higher Secondary Certificate.

Admission Procedure

At the secondary level, admissions are made twice a year, first in May-June and then in December-January at the Study Centres spread all over West Bengal. At the Senior Secondary level, registration of students is made once a year in the month of July-August.

Enrolment

Inception of RMV is quite recent. It started enrolling its students from 2000-2001. In December 2003-04, the registered number of total students at the secondary stage were 23575, and at the senior secondary stage 1187. The enrolment data (Table 5.15) show that the number of students joining RMV for secondary and senior secondary courses is continuously increasing. Up to 2001 RMV was running only secondary level courses. From 2002 it started senior secondary level courses. The break-up of enrolment at secondary and senior secondary levels also shows the increasing demand of these courses. During 2001-02, the percentage increase at the secondary level was 287.39, while at the senior secondary level it was 278.70 in 2002-03. This remarkably significant rise in enrolment may be attributed primarily to the policy of decentralisation of admissions through the network of study centres and secondly to the rigorous efforts made by RMV to develop linkages with formal education system, particularly the examination boards and universities that have accorded recognition and equivalent status to RMV certification. In addition to organisational aspects, its quality of content and process can be held responsible for its credibility and increase in student strength. RMV gets appropriate self-learning materials prepared by subject-experts, publishes them and makes them available to the learners through their respective study centres. In addition, RMV allows its students to take examinations in a phased manner according to their own pace of preparation and convenience. They are given nine chances over a span of five years to clear the full secondary course with credit-accumulation facility.

Table 5.15: Number of Students at the Secondary and Senior Secondary Level, RMV, Kolkata

Year	*Secondary*	*% Increase*	*Higher Secondary*	*% Increase*
2000-01	3314	–	–	–
2001-02	12838	287.39	338	–
2002-03	20868	62.55	1280	278.70
2003-04	23575	12.97	1187	–.07

Source: Rabindra Mukta Vidhyalaya, Salt Lake, Kolkata.

Study Material and Counseling

RMV imparts open learning through self-study materials and personal contact programmes. Part-time learners of the open system have to depend mainly on self-study. Designing materials for this purpose has developed into a highly specialised job. RMV gets appropriate study materials specially designed and prepared for self-learning by subject-experts and experienced teachers. It publishes the materials and makes them available to the learners through their respective study centres. Students get the study materials of the subjects offered by them through their Study Centres immediately after registration free of cost. Study Centres engage qualified teaching staff with the approval of RMV who conducts counseling through personal contact programmes. Counseling is given on Saturdays, Sundays or any other holidays. The Study Centres are mostly located at Government aided Secondary/Higher Secondary Schools spread all over West Bengal. A few of them run in non-governmental organisations also. During 2003-04, the total number of accredited Study Centres rose from 57 to 125 and Higher Secondary Study Centres from 23 to 42.

Examination System

RMV conducts external examinations through its network of Study Centres spread all over West Bengal. With the sharp increase in the number of students, there has also been a steady increase in the number of examination centres, from 42 centres in 1999-2000 to 104 centres in 2002-03. The students enrolled in a particular Study Centre have to sit for their examination in another Study Centre. Conducting examination is a big task that is handled meticulously by RMV twice every year.

In order to lighten the load of several subjects at a time, RMV allows its students to take examination in a phased manner according to their preparation and at their own convenient place. The evaluation of the answer books is organised in selected centres in the state. Most of the evaluators are teachers from formal schools that have been trained and oriented in the RMV marking scheme. At each evaluation centre a co-coordinator is appointed by RMV to oversee the overall procedure of the evaluation. After having computerised the marks, RMV declares the results within two months. The mark-sheets as well as the migration certificates of the successful candidates are sent along with results' gazette to the study centres.

Table 5.16 throws light on the current enrolment in the Secondary and Senior Secondary school examinations. The enrolment of female students is higher than that of male students at the secondary level, but the case reverses in the senior secondary stage.

Table 5.16: Examination Results of Secondary and Senior Secondary Schools RMV, Kolkata, 2003

Particulars	*Secondary*	*Senior Secondary*
Registered No. of examinees	5454	384
Out of all Subjects total no. appeared	3968	68*
Of these successful candidates	1710	27
First Div	98	1
Second Div	818	17
Third Div	794	9
Of All Successful Candidates		
Male	918	18
Female	792	9

Source: Rabindra Mukta Vidhyalaya, Salt Lake, Kolkata.
* Out of all subjects, minimum number of students in at least three subjects.

Tables 5.17 and 5.18 give a picture of subject-wise performance of students at the secondary and senior secondary levels. The pass percentage is high in all subjects, except English, at both the levels, which determines the higher turnout of students. It can be concluded that since the pass percentage of the students is quite high, it can attract more students in future because this correspondence course not only gives them flexibility of time but also of attempts. The course can prove to be an inspiring success after some years.

Table 5.17: Number of Registered, Appeared and Pass Percentage of Students

Subjects	*Registered*	*Appeared*	*Passed*	*Pass %*
Bengali	3126	2881	2117	73.48
English	3935	3744	2089	55.80
Math	3284	3030	2001	66.04
Physics	3538	3298	2025	61.40
Biology	2950	2716	1985	73.09
Geography	2946	2732	2271	83.13
History	3371	3116	2443	78.40
Home Science	323	296	286	96.62
Political Science	66	60	48	80.00
Economics	13	11	9	81.82
Commerce	23	18	14	77.78

Source: Rabindra Mukta Vidhyalaya, Salt Lake, Kolkata.

Table 5.18: Number of Registered, Appeared and Pass Percentage of Students

Subjects	*Registered*	*Appeared*	*Passed*	*Pass %*
Bengali	307	267	228	85.39
English	230	207	115	55.56
History	208	189	150	79.37
Political Science	174	153	123	80.39
Education	147	120	116	96.67
Economic Geography	78	67	62	92.54
Business Organisation and Enterprise	23	20	18	90
Accountancy	20	17	15	88.24

Source: Rabindra Mukta Vidhyalaya, Salt Lake, Kolkata.

In addition there may be other students qualifying in one or more subjects and since they accumulate the credits, it cannot be treated as failure. It is difficult to know how much students have spent time in the system. Most of the students who received certificates were able to complete the course over two years. Despite the flexibility offered by RMV, most of the students opt to take either all subjects or more than three or four subjects at a time. This leads to high rate of failures. Also a large number of RMV clientele belongs to the category of drop-outs, rural and working people, and the disadvantaged and women, who fail to complete the course for different reasons. They have low academic standard. Though PCP provide counseling and guidance to the students in planning their studies, but the support that the students get from PCPs is not at all satisfactory. Some ardent protagonists of open school regret that PCPs, instead of being exercises in tutoring 'counseling and mentoring', actually take the shape of conventional lecture classes. These classes are large in number and are precisely not what these part-time students require. Counseling and mentoring make little sense to them. In addition, it is undeniable that the study centres have very little option in this matter. The teachers are confronted with the formidable task of helping a heterogeneous group of students having his/her own problems in different subjects. The next day same teachers may face another group of learners, again heterogeneous in character, with different queries. On the contrary, in the formal schools, by allotting specific periods for different subjects where instead of attempting to meet individual queries teachers find it fruitful to discuss the topics following the syllabus.

Recognition of RMV Certificate

Giving due recognition to the open system, the Government of West Bengal has accepted RMV's secondary and senior secondary certificates as equivalent to those of the WBBSE and WBCHSE respectively. Several state universities have also declared open school pass-outs as eligible in their undergraduate courses.

Expenditure

As mentioned earlier, RMV imparts open learning through self-study materials and personal contact programmes. Part-time learners of the open system have to depend mainly on self-study. Therefore, expenditure is highest in preparation of the study materials (40.90 per cent), followed by conduct of examinations (15.18 per cent), and recognition of study centres covered by only .22 per cent.

Role of Board in Quality Improvement and Change

RMV was established with the aim of providing education to the people who could not avail the opportunity of having education at their proper age and cannot do so even now because of socio-economic and various other hurdles. How far RMV has been successful in achieving this objective? Views of the Chairman of the Board (RMV), Prof Ranju Gopal Mukhopadhyay were taken on the functioning of the RMV through a structured questionnaire.

RMV plays a key role in the open learning system in spreading education. RMV still has to generate necessary public awareness or interest about its mission and activities. In fact, it has shied away from publicity. They think that further increase in the number of centres and learners may lead to mismanagement. They still have to make use of modern information and communication technology for imparting instructions. Application of computers, TVs and other electronic media, would enhance quality of teaching. RMV has not yet adopted such programmes.

At present, RMV, like WBBSE and WBCHSE, is providing all the routine activities but on a much smaller scale but with large variety. It has to take into consideration that whatever the volume may be, functions like preparing curricula and syllabi, granting affiliation to study centres and monitoring their performance, holding public examinations and publishing results etc. involve the same procedure. Introduction of vocational courses and holding of 8th class public examination is in the pipeline. However, RMV has a skeleton of staff that too on hire. It is grappling with its current activities on the strength of an honorary Chairman, a Director and only eleven other sanctioned posts, for nine of which the condition is that these should have to be filled up with retired persons on contract basis. There are only one group C and one group D posts. There is no post in the field of finance and accounts, although the RMV handles public money and is required under the law to prepare budgets and get its accounts audited.

Therefore, government needs to take note of RMV's essential requirements and give its due priority in plans. It needs personnel who can render services on long time basis. Frequent change of personnel hampers continuity of ideas, policies and orientation.

Open learning at school level has a very important role to play in extending educational opportunities to those deprived people who, because of age, occupation or any other hurdle, are not in a position to take advantage of the formal system. But its scope should not be extended to out-of-school children of normal school-going age who fully deserve the same formal schooling facility as enjoyed by their more fortune counterparts (Report of the School Education Committee, West Bengal, 2002).

6

Board of Secondary Education Andhra Pradesh

Board of Secondary Education, Andhra Pradesh (AP), was established in 1953, under Andhra Education Act, 1952 and the Board conducted the first SSC public examination in 1955.

In AP, the function of school education system is bifurcated into three departments, i.e., Directorate of School Education, SCERT, and Board of Secondary Education. Directorate of School Education looks after educational administration, inspection, supervision and management. The academic matters, such as development of curriculum, professional guidelines, research, preparation of teaching and learning material are the responsibility of SCERT. The Board of Secondary Education is concerned with evaluation of the performance of students.

The Board is under the state government control. It does not have full autonomy. An officer from the Department of Education holds the office of the Director of Examination. Presently, Dr. D. Ravinranadham is the head of the Department. During 2002-03, around 6.64 lakhs students of Class 10 from over 11000 secondary schools in the State appeared in the Secondary School Certificate (SSC) examination. The number of total working days in AP schools is 220 days. Out of it, 180 days are devoted to imparting instructions and 30 days are kept for examinations. Generally, schools work for 5 to 6 hours per day. The Board organises examinations in March and October every year, but at present supplementary examination is held within a month after declaration of SSC examination result.

The Board adheres to the norms of opening, recognition and affiliation of schools as laid down by the Directorate of Education. In AP, 72.92 per cent of population lives in rural areas (Census 2001).

Therefore, to bridge the disparity of rural and urban areas, government opens maximum number of schools in the remote and difficult areas according to the requirement.

Organisational Set-up

Director is the head of the Board of Secondary Education. Three Deputy Commissioners and 12 Assistant Commissioners for Government Examinations (ACGEs) assist him at the headquarters. In addition, there are 23 ACGEs who are assisted by 46 Superintendents, 85 Senior Assistants, 82 Junior Assistants, and 72 secretarial and Group D staff, either at the headquarters or under the control of District Education Officers in the State (see Figure 6.1).

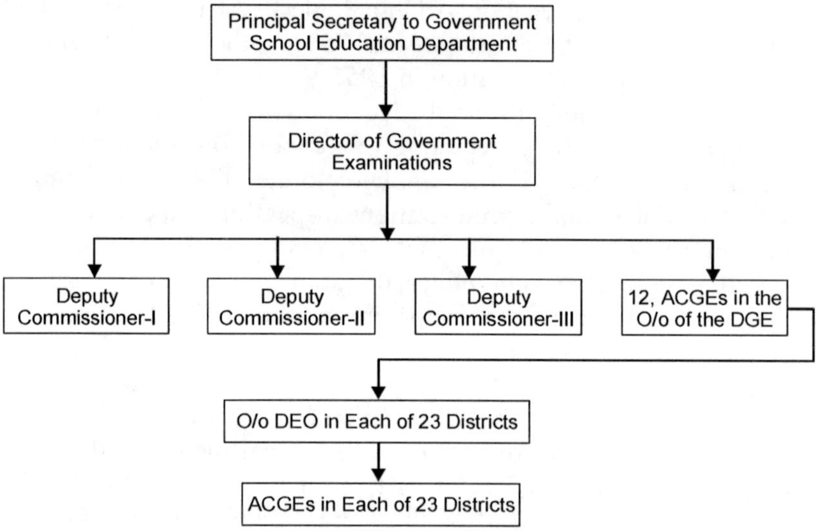

Fig. 6.1: Organisational Set-Up of the Directorate of Government Examinations, Andhra Pradesh

Functions of the Board

The main role of Board, according to Act, is to conduct public examinations, particularly at the terminal stages of VII and X standards and issue of certificates. The Board is also entrusted with the conduct of various other examinations of professional courses, such as Elementary Teacher Training (ETT), Diploma in Education

(D.Ed.), Pandit Training Courses (PTC), etc. and issue of certificates for all these courses.

Broadly in terms of priority, these functions can be stated as follows:

- To advise the government on issue of coordinated development of secondary education;
- To formulate schemes for conducting examinations;
- To conduct examinations of standard X and other teacher training courses;
- To award certificates to X Class pass-outs and for teacher training courses;
- To make recommendations to government with regard to:
    - (i) Course of study and medium of instruction;
    - (ii) Syllabi and curriculum for various courses of study;
    - (iii) Fixation of fees and other charges for examinations; and
    - (iv) Standards of achievement in various subjects to qualify for promotion and award of certificates.

To carry out the above functions, the Board constitutes: (i) Academic, and (ii) Examination Committees.

(i) Academic Committee advises the Board on academic policies or introduction of new courses of study and new combination of subjects.

(ii) Examination Committee helps the Board with regard to matters related to examinations like structure of question papers, nature of test items and norms to deal with cases of malpractices in examinations.

As the Board's major function is to conduct examinations, therefore all the staff members are involved the whole year in the examination related work. Mapping of examination work is made like: (a) From October to May—preparation and conduct of examination work, and (b) from June to September—analysis and review of examination papers for improving the qualitative achievement level of students.

Since the Board is mainly concerned with public examinations, it has taken major decisions to render examinations more reliable, credible and free from malpractices. To make the administration transparent and unbiased, the system is computerised. Bar code system is adopted. Access by students, parents and others is made easier with the setting up of the website of the Board, and through e-mail communication etc.

In Andhra Pradesh, there is a well-knit coordination between the Directorate of Education, SCERT, and the Board. The Board of Secondary Education gives its recommendation regarding analysis of students' results to these departments for quality improvement of schools accordingly either for Directorate or SCERT to take actions.

Academic Functions

Curriculum Updation

In AP, curriculum updation is looked after by SCERT, but the Board advises the government on academic policies and introduction of new courses of study and new combination of subjects. After about every ten years the curriculum is updated in a phased manner from Class 1 to Class 10 as per the guidelines issued by NCERT's National Curriculum Framework for School Education (2000). While updating the curriculum, special care is taken for education for girls, learners with special needs, disadvantaged groups as well as gifted and talented students.

Responding to the impact of globalisation, various changes have been incorporated in the curriculum like introduction of education concerning active citizenship and human rights, environmental issues, universal values, etc. and teaching material has also been developed in these areas.

Reducing Curriculum Load on Students

To reduce the curriculum load on students, SCERT changes some of the parts of curriculum and textbooks every year and reprints of chapters deleted and added are brought out. The changes are brought on the basis of representations received from the teachers, teacher organisations, parents, students and general public.

Availability of Subjects

All the schools affiliated to the Board of Secondary Education have common syllabus. Core subjects are same for all the students at the secondary level. Mathematics, Science and Social Studies with three languages are the compulsory subjects. Thus the students have to study six subjects, i.e., three subjects under languages and three non-language subjects. Apart from this, students can opt for one subject from Life Skill subjects list.

Life Skills Education

At the secondary level, under Life Skills Education, vocational courses are introduced. These courses have been introduced in a selected number of schools in certain trades, according to the need of the region. Through Life Skills Education students get training in various trades. At present, training is available in 15 trades. The students have a choice to select one or two trades from the list of the trades available for study. The students have to appear in the examination for the academic courses along with Life Skills subjects. The students, who opt for these subjects, are given two certifications, one in academic and other in Life Skills Education or Vocational Course.

While developing the curriculum for Life Skills subjects or vocational education, the varying needs of not only the girls, SC/STs and physically challenged persons, but also those of the communities living in rural/urban areas and in different geographical locations are taken into consideration and developed accordingly, making the choice available to the students to select the vocation as per their specific needs and requirements.

Textbooks

The AP Textbook Press prints and distributes books from Classes I to X in Telugu, English, Urdu and Hindi languages. In addition the press also prints books in minority languages, like Marathi, Oriya, Kannada and Tamil. At present, books are distributed free of cost to SC, ST, BC and physically handicapped students studying in Classes VI to X.

Steps Taken in Context of Erosion of Social, Moral and Spiritual Values

Keeping in view the erosion of essential social, moral and spiritual values, detailed curricula and syllabi have been developed in 'moral education'. It is a compulsory subject from Class I to Class X. In addition, while writing the textbooks for all subjects; special care is taken to integrate the values to be inculcated among the children with the content matter of the course. All teachers in the state are also given orientation courses in integrating these values through teaching-learning practice and various activities introduced in the schools. Special programmes, such as symposia, conferences, and seminars are conducted on the development of essential values among the students.

Instructional Techniques

School curriculum is transacted through various instructional materials like textbooks, workbooks, teacher's handbooks and multimedia material. The textbooks are used to cover the syllabus. These are used as reference material for teachers and reading material for students. Workbook is used for development of various abilities among the students and for continuous evaluation of progress of the students. The usage of workbook is also useful for providing remedial teaching after identifying the common mistakes. Workbooks have been developed for all the classes in English language subject and for primary classes these are developed for non-language subjects with the initiative of DPEP. Teacher handbooks are developed and used by the teachers for professional growth, content development, updating the teaching skills so as to make the classroom transaction more interesting and motivating for students.

Multimedia material is used in classroom process to develop various skills, like thinking, learning abilities, creativity, etc. Multimedia is also used to achieve the aims of globalisation of education for developing learning abilities and to involve the students in teaching-learning process.

At the secondary stage, learner-centered approach is being followed, in addition to involving the students in different activities of the schools by introducing discussion method. The students are also taken on educational tours, and field trips. All the schools organise Art and Science exhibitions involving the students. In addition, to bring change in teaching-learning process with the modern educational technology schools have been supplied with televisions, tape recorders etc. Moreover, computer education has also been introduced in the pre-service teacher education programmes in the schools to bring in awareness of the information technology and integrate its use with education.

ICT and Professional Growth of Teachers

Information Communication Technology (ICT) has been used in transacting curriculum of pre-service teacher education programmes, like preparation of lesson plans, acquiring additional knowledge and information, obtaining latest statistics and its implications, global developments in different subjects, and modern evaluation techniques, etc. In the schools, efforts have also been made to develop computer labs for extensive use of ICT for professional growth of teachers providing quality education to students and to achieve globalisation of education.

Monitoring of Schools

Monitoring of schools is done by the Directorate of Education with the help of District Education Officers (DEO). The DEOs of the zone consisting of about 40 to 50 schools inspect the schools and arrange discussions with the selected senior and experienced head masters in difficult school subjects and academic problems. The experts provide academic guidance after supervising the academic work done by the schools and follow-up visits are also made to review the implementation of the guidance given.

Conduct of Examinations

Functions of the Examination Committee are: to conduct public examinations; to release results as per time schedule; and to issue pass Certificates and failed Memos. Primarily, the Board conducts Class VII and Secondary School Certificate examinations. After declaration of SSC examination result, it conducts within one-month supplementary examination. Total number of examinations conducted by the Board is as follows:

1. SSC Public Examinations
2. SSC Vocational Examinations
3. VII Class Vocational Examinations
4. First Year (Diploma in Education) Examinations
5. 2nd Year (D.Ed.) Examinations
6. Pre-Primary Teacher Training Certificate (PPTTC) Public Examinations
7. CLISc Public Examinations
8. Headmaster Accountant Test
9. Telugu Pandits Training Examinations
10. Urdu Pandits Training Examinations
11. Hindi Pandits Training Examinations
12. Sanskrit Entrance Examinations
13. Professional Advancement Test for Teachers

14. National Talent Search Examinations
15. Teachers Technical Certificate (TTC) Examination (42 days course)
16. Technical Certificate Course Examination

In addition to conducting public examinations and releasing their results, the Department delivers the following services:

(a) Issue of Duplicate Pass Certificate – within one week to the school concerned
(b) Issue of Compartmental Pass Certificate – within ten days to the school concerned
(c) Issue of Duplicate Memos, Age and Migration Certificates—within two days
(d) Re-counting of Marks – within twenty days
(e) Corrections in Certificate – within three days
(f) Verification of Certificates – within one week
(g) Deciding withheld cases – within ten days
(h) Disposal of Malpractice Cases – within one month from the date of publication of results
(i) Age Condonations – within five days
(j) Permission to outside candidates to appear for SSC Exams/ VII Class Exams – within a week
(k) Concession to Physically Handicapped Candidates

For conducting the above examinations, the Board follows the following steps:

- Issue of notification for the conduct of SSC Examinations.
- Fixation of fees structure.
- Issue of instructions to Heads of Institutions for preparation of Nominal Roll and Application Forms/ICR Forms.
- Collecting filled in ICR (Integrated Computerised Registration) forms and computer processing.
- Constitution of examination centres.
- Distribution of hall-tickets.
- Question paper setting/moderation.
- Transportation of question papers and examination material to the examination centres.
- Transportation of examination related stationery, i.e., blank answer books and additional books to the examination centres.

- Issue of instructions to various functionaries of the District Administration in the State in connection with the conduct of examinations.
- Coordination with other Departments, such as Revenue, Police, Health and Postal Department, with regard to conduct of examinations.
- Conduct of district-wise spot valuation camps to evaluate answer scripts.
- Preparation and distribution of principles of valuation/key to the spot valuation centres.
- Release of Result.
- Issue of pass certificate and fail memos.
- Preparation of statistics and analysis of results.
- Assessment of results
- Identifying high performing schools, low performing schools and zero percentage schools.
- Furnishing of report to the Government on low performing schools and zero percentage schools for remedial measures.
- Issue of duplicate pass certificates to the candidates who have completed the examination in different sittings.
- Issue of compartmental pass certificates to the candidates who have completed the examination in different sittings.
- To settle the withheld cases of candidates whose results at the public examination are withheld due to various reasons.
- Recording of marks by calling for the answer scripts from the spot valuation camps for scrutiny and to intimate changes.
- Award medals/mementos to meritorious candidates.

Paper Setting

The teachers do examination paper setting and moderation work. Translations of papers are made by professors and lecturers. Every year 280 to 300 teachers are involved in paper setting and 30 to 34 teachers for moderation. The Board officials felt the need of training for paper setters, moderators, evaluators and related members so that measures can be taken in time to overcome the shortcoming and the enhance the quality of the entrusted work.

Examination Centres

Generally, examination centres are created at suitable places by

Examination Committee of the Board. Examination centres are decided at least three months before the examination by the competent authority. While deciding the examination centre, care is taken by the authorities that selected centre is such that some check can be put at the entry point, in order that malpractices can be controlled to a great extent. The supervisors are from a distant place who do not have any axe to grind against the institution to whom the examinees belong. The apprehension in the mind of the examinees as well as the institutions should not be there that the observers and supervisors are acting with an attitude of bias.

Table 6.1 shows the number of schools and the number of examination centres and their ratio. From the table we learn that the total number of schools increased from 9,260 in 2000-01 to 12,153 in 2003-04 and the examination centres increased from 2,590 in 2000-01 to 3,265 in 2003-04. The number of schools increased faster than the number of centres. The percentage increase in the number of schools was 31.25 from 2000-01 to 2003-04 and the percentage increase in examination centres was 26.06. However, the ratio among the schools and examination centres was almost the same.

Table 6.1: Number of Schools and Examination Centres

	No. of Schools	*No. of Examination Cetnres*	*Ratio*
2000-01	9260	2590	3.5
2001-02	10273	2752	3.7
2002-03	11056	3013	3.6
2003-04	12153	3265	3.7
% increase	31.24	26.06	–

Major Examination Reforms

Non-detention System

In AP, non-detention system has been introduced except for Classes VII and X. However, evaluation procedure has been strengthened by conducting monthly unit tests and periodical examinations such as quarterly, half-yearly and annual examinations to maintain quality education.

Continuous and Comprehensive Evaluation

Continuous and comprehensive evaluation is carried out in all the schools at all the stages of education through:

- Oral examination;
- Oral exam during teaching-learning process;
- Observation of students work in the library, in the laboratory, in the playground and in the school, particularly in different activities in the school;
- Entrusting certain activities and assignments to the students;
- Terminal examinations; and
- Interaction with parents during PTA meetings.

Using Unfair Means

If a student is caught in the examination hall while copying, it becomes a legal issue, which is tackled by the examination purification committee. On being found guilty, he/she is debarred from appearing at the next examinations for a period deemed fit by the committee. But suspect student is given opportunity to defend himself/herself. This practice is applicable where a few students indulge in malpractice. But in a situation where lot of students indulges in mass copying, authorities on enquiry have every right to cancel the examination held. In such cases they can take two types of actions: Re-examination—where students are involved in mass copying the authorities may cancel the results of all the students or they may not conduct re-examination and award zero marks to all the students. In such a situation a few students who may not have been involved in malpractice, are also affected. Examination cancelled without notice—the authorities may cancel the examinations without notice to the examinees who had appeared at the centre. However, this type of action is taken before the publication of results.

Supplementary Examination

Andhra Pradesh Board conducts supplementary examination within one month after declaring public examination results. The results of supplementary examinations are declared within 10 days so that students do not lose an academic year.

Re-evaluation

Re-counting of marks in the public examinations is allowed while re-evaluation of answer-books is not allowed. Where a student is declared successful after re-evaluation, his application for admission in the next higher class cannot be rejected on the ground that the last date for admission has expired.

In short, following quality improvement related functions have been adopted by the Board in the examinations:

- Periodic achievement surveys;
  - — Conduct of unit tests in all subjects, by subject teachers with a view to taking up remedial teaching to keep the parents informed of the progress of the wards;
  - — Conduct of Quarterly, Half-Yearly and Annual examinations for which question papers are set by the District Common Examination Boards;
- Maintenance of comprehensive progress report by the schools for each and every student and communicating it to the parents;
- Involving students in the teaching-learning process by putting questions to the students and encouraging them to put questions to the teacher to get their doubts cleared;
- Organising co-curricular activities by the teachers;
- For non-cognitive areas, grading system has been introduced; and
- More internal choice is provided in question papers so that all levels of students, such as backward, average, intelligent, etc. are able to answer the questions.

Students Performance

Table 6.2 shows performance of boys and girl students for ten years from 1992-93 to 2002-03. Table indicates three things. First, number of both the boys and girls appearing for Board examinations at secondary level has successively increased (2.67 lakh to 3.73 lakh boys and 1.57 lakh to 2.91 lakh girls). Second, the number of girls appearing in examination has increased at a much faster rate than Boys. The percentage of girls appearing in exams has increased to 85 while that of boys increased to 40 from the year 1993-94 to 2002-03. Third, the performance of boys and girls in the Board examinations is almost equal.

Table 6.2: Performance of Students at Secondary Level

Year	*Appeared*		*Pass Percentage*	
	Boys	*Girls*	*Boys*	*Girls*
1993-94	267643	157024	48.01	49.76
1994-95	261978	160646	59.10	60.17
1995-96	274192	173824	58.28	57.88
1996-97	286183	185710	55.81	55.56
1997-98	289477	194492	46.52	47.12
1998-99	286269	198117	53.34	53.57
1999-2000	303488	217153	54.18	54.90
2000-01	331673	242882	64.75	65.61
2001-02	350647	266211	68.06	67.66
2002-03	373712	291242	75.04	74.94
% increased from 1993-94 to 2002-03	39.63	85.48		

In Andhra Pradesh, more than 70 per cent population lives in rural areas. Table 6.3 substantiates the fact. In all categories of schools in rural areas the number of appeared students is more. The highest number of students is from zilla parishad rural schools and the lowest number of students who appeared in the SSC examination is from residential rural schools (300988 students' zilla parishad rural schools and 9031 students from residential rural schools). The analysis shows that generally students opt for either government schools or zilla parishad schools. Performance of students is highest in residential rural schools as well as residential urban schools; it is followed by private schools and zilla parishad schools.

Table 6.3: Performance of Students (2002-03)

Type of School	*Appeared*	*Passed*	*Pass %*
Govt. Rural	47633	31332	65.77
Govt. Urban	9650	4906	50.83
Zilla Parishad Rural	300988	223478	74.24
Zilla Parishad Urban	14904	10734	72.02
Muncipal Rural	11937	6570	55.03
Muncipal Urban	3198	1946	60.85
Residential Rural	9031	8420	93.23
Residential Urban	2123	1922	90.53
Private Rural	194567	157483	80.94
Private Urban	68840	50305	70.07

Sources of Income

The Board's main sources of income are grants from the government and fees from examinations. Board's income does not accrue from other sources such as donations, endowment, royalty etc. Table 6.4 indicates that during a span of eight years, i.e., 1995-96 to 2003-04, income from government sources increased by 165.68 per cent and income from examination fees increased by 172.55 per cent.

Table 6.4: Source of Income of Board of Secondary Education (Rs. in Lakhs)

Year	*Grants from Government*	*Examinations*
1995-96	1130.69	1151.55
2001-02	2086.16	2593.21
2002-03	2462.71	2751.34
2003-04	3004.08	3138.58
% increase	165.68	172.55

Examination Fees

Three types of examination fees are charged for three types of students, i.e., regular students, private students who failed once, for private students who never attended schools and are appearing in SSC examinations. From 1995-96 to 2003-04, examination fees have increased from Rs. 45 to Rs. 100 for regular students. Private students (once failed) earlier had to pay Rs. 35 for upto 3 subject during 1995-96; it has now been increased to Rs. 90 in 2003-04. Third category is of private students, who have not attended any schools. They have to pay an examination fee Rs. 45 and in addition Rs. 150 as attendance exemption fee. These have now been increased to Rs. 85 (examination fees) and Rs. 350 as examination exemption fee. Penalties charged for delays in payment was Rs. 3 for one week; it has been increased to Rs. 10; for the 2nd week, it has been increased from Rs. 33 to Rs. 40. Earlier, after the 3rd week, students were not eligible for submitting the form, but from 2001-02 a provision for late fee of Rs. 100 has been also provided to such students. They can submit their form after paying Rs. 100 as late fee (see Table 6.5). Re-evaluation fee has increased from Rs. 50 to Rs. 75 during the selected period.

Table 6.5: Examination Fees in Secondary Stage (in Rs)

Examination Fees	*1995-96*	*2001-02*	*2003-04*
Regular students	45	85	100
Private students (once failed)			
Upto 3 subjects	35	80	90
Private students (without school study)	45 + attendance exemption fee 150	45 + attendance exemption fee 350	85 + attendance exemption fee 350
Penalties charged for delays			
For 1st week	3	10	10
For 2nd week	33	40	40
For 3rd week	-	100	100
Re-Evaluation Fee	50	75	75

No fee is charged from weaker sections of students. According to government's instructions, Social Welfare Department has to reimburse the fee amount to students whose parents' income is below Rs. 12,000 per annum. According to the Board officials, it is not in practice and roughly 40-45 per cent students are not paying the fees.

Table 6.6 shows that during a span of six years, i.e., from 1995-96 to 2001-02, there has been not much difference in remuneration charges for various examination related activities, except of head examiner's remuneration. Head examiner's remuneration has been increased from Rs. 80 to Rs. 140.

Table 6.6: Expenditure on Conduct of Examination (in Rs)

Remuneration Charges	*1995-96*	*2001-02*
Paper setters	200	200
Moderators	200	200
Head examiners	80	140
Examiners	2.25 per valued answer script	3 per valued answer script
Invigilators	12 per day	12 per day

Table 6.7: Comparative Picture of Income and Expenditure (Rs. in lakhs)

Year	*Income*	*Expenditure*	*Surplus/Deficit*
2001-02	1883	2059	-176
2003-03	2751	2754	-003
2003-04	2900	3000	-100

The main function of the Board is to conduct examinations. Table 6.8 indicates that during 1995-96, major expenditure of Rs. 8966 lakhs was on examination related activities. But over the years the expenditure on examinations has decreased. In 2002-03, the expenditure on examinations was reduced to Rs. 1399 lakhs, which increased to Rs. 2130 lakhs in 2003-04. On the other hand expenditure on staff salary and publications has increased. Staff salary increased more than two times from 1995-96 to 2003-04, and expenditure on publications increased more than four times during the same period.

Table 6.8: Items of Expenditure (in Rs. lakhs)

Year	*Staff Salary*	*Examination*	*Publication*
1995-96	1120	8966	1220
2001-02	2941	1653	1382
2002-03	304	1399	2500
2003-04	2449	2130	5410

Interaction with Board Officials

To understand the philosophy, working, and perception about school education and to know how accordingly changes are made in the policies and practices of the Board, following Board officials were interviewed:

Director Examination	Dr. D. Ravindranadnam
Deputy Commissioner	Shri Surya Prakash
Deputy Commissioner	Shri Pawan Kumar
Deputy Commissioner	Shri Rangacharya

The discussion with the Director Dr. D. Ravindranadnam and other officials revealed that four types of innovations have been incorporated in the education system in Andhra Pradesh.

Text-books Updation

SCERT looks after the development of curriculum. The Director SCERT has got the freedom for adding or deleting any chapters in the textbooks for schools. Every year, reprints of the added chapters are brought out. This effort saves the time and money if the entire textbook incorporating the changes has not to be brought out.

Introduction of Life Skills Education

At the secondary level, students have to opt for three compulsory subjects and three optional subjects. In addition, according to the needs of regions, 17 Life Skills (vocational courses) have been introduced, related to different trades. Students who opt for these subjects or vocational courses have to appear in the examination along with the academic courses. In the vocational courses, students have to complete projects with the help of teachers and headmasters; thus they get practical training in vocational courses.

Status of Computerisation

In the Board, computerisation has taken place only for processing examination data, tabulation of data and issue of mark-sheets and certificates to students. The employees' records, salary bills, etc. are not computerised yet.

Coordination and Linkage with All Educational Departments

In Andhra Pradesh all the educational organisations or departments are headed by 'Educational Service People'. Therefore, all the educational organisations have coordination and linkage among them. For example, results of the Board are analysed by the AP Board of Secondary Education. The schools, which are below expected levels (with 0-20 per cent result), are identified and report is sent to the Directorate of Education. The Directorate, through monitoring and supervision, identifies the reasons and training of teachers is imparted accordingly through SCERT.

Computerisation of Examination Result

The Board has completely computerised the examination results, including its management so as to enhance quality and efficiency in the system. Examination data is processed by computer agencies. To maintain the secrecy, stickers are pasted on the enrolment of the students. Within three weeks after examination the results are declared. Re-evaluation of examination is also conducted within one month after declaration of the results so that pass students are able to seek admission into the next class in the same academic year.

Sharing of Examination Results

Every year the Board does comparative analyses of students' performance in public examinations through various ways, like management-wise schools; Government schools, Private schools, Municipality schools, Residential schools, and girls and boys schools. Also subject-wise performance is evaluated. Thereafter a meeting of the District Education Officers and Principals of schools is organised and those schools whose results are below the expected levels are exhorted to improve the result. After that, the principals hold meetings of the teachers in this connection and adopt corrective measures by addressing the hard points of students' learning in the subject concerned.

Announcement of Results

The Board announces results for the SSC examinations through various modes, like newspapers, gazettes, on the websites of the Board 'www.aponline.gov.nic.in' and 'www.aponline.gov.in'. The results are also tied up with other government electronic media, like BSNL, interactive voice response system (IVRS), and other private telecom companies like IDEA, Airtel, Hutch, etc.

Capacity Building Programmes for Experienced Principals

SCERT conducts orientation programmes for experienced principals, to keep them abreast of the developments in the field of education, modern trends in evaluation, pedagogy, etc.

Capacity Building Programmes for Newly Recruited Teachers

Newly recruited teachers are given orientation in the subject they have to teach. They are also called to the teachers' centre periodically to get their doubts cleared. The Heads of Institutions develop confidence in them by motivating them in staff meetings. They are attached to the senior teachers in the respective subjects to provide continuous guidance. The Head of Institutions observes the classroom teaching and provides necessary help and guidance. The inspecting officers, during their periodical visits to the school, pay attention to the newly recruited teachers and provide all necessary academic support to build up their confidence.

Preparation of Modules

For certain textbooks, modular packages have been developed.

However, efforts are being taken by the DPEP and SCERT to prepare complete modular packages of the textbooks and workbooks.

Orientation Materials for Parents, Community Members

Whenever meetings, seminars, workshops are organised, orientation materials are developed and circulated to teachers on the various policies, practices, programmes of the government and on effective curriculum transaction techniques for quality education. Also material is developed for parents and community members to keep them abreast with the government policies and programmes.

Recommendations

- The Board of Secondary Education should be given administrative and financial powers not only for strengthening the Board but also to bring in smooth functioning and monitoring to achieve quality in education.
- There is need to remodel the Board, expanding the functions and scope for introducing innovative modern evaluation practices to achieve quality in education. To achieve these objectives, it may be necessary to make the Board an autonomous organisation.
- Need for modification in the curriculum to attract the students from other states as well as from other countries. For that the Board of Secondary Education needs to identify the special needs of those children and develop curriculum specially suitable to their needs.
- Need to build linkages between schools and industries. Therefore, while developing the curriculum and syllabus, and writing of textbooks, the personnel from different industries, institutes, have also to be involved.
- Need to incorporate changes in the instructional pattern to meet the challenge of impact of globalisation.
- Need to impart pre-service training to principals. Though, SCERT at the state level and in collaboration with the Board of Secondary Education and the Directorate of School Education imparts training as and when budget provision is available, but there is need to systematise and institutionalise the training.

7

Quality Secondary Education for Global Competitiveness

Conclusions

Comparative Scenario of Secondary Education in Four States

The study of all the state Boards gives us an idea that all the Secondary Education Boards in the four States work around the respective legislature/regulatory 'Acts' and consider these 'Acts' as Bible. Further, most of their time is consumed on examination activities.

Medium of Instruction

In all the Boards studied, the medium of instruction is the regional language or the state language, along with Hindi/English as the national language. Third language is from the list of several Indian and foreign languages.

The language formula adopted is according to the recommendations of the Kothari Commission. Kothari Commission was set up to review the entire education system. Two recommendations of the Kothari Commission can be quoted here. One pertains to the 10+2 structure of education at the school level. Under this structure 12 years schooling has been divided into several sub-stages, i.e., Pre-Primary, Primary, Upper Primary, Secondary and Senior Secondary level. Second recommendation suggests 3-language formula at the secondary level. Students up to secondary level are required to learn three languages. All the Boards in the four states have adopted this recommendation with some modifications according to their own priorities. In West Bengal Board of Secondary Education (WBBSE), the third language is taught only in Classes VII and VIII.

Decentralisation

Keeping in view the large number of students at the secondary and senior secondary level, in West Bengal, WBBSE and WBCHSE and in Madhya Pradesh, the Board of Secondary Education (BSEMP) have decentralised their activities. WBBSE and WBCHSE have established 4 regional offices, and BSEMP has established 7 divisional Boards to cater to the needs of students residing in those areas.

Headquarters of Boards

According to the Act of the Boards' headquarters should be located at a place, which is conveniently accessible to the public, students and teachers. The place should be suitable from the point of view of administrative convenience, employees' interest and for liaison with the State Government offices.

It has been found that all the Boards except the Himachal Pradesh School Education Board (HPSEB) are located at the capital cities of the respective states. In the beginning, HPSEB was established in the capital city of Himachal Pradesh, i.e., Shimla. Since the weather in Shimla is extremely cold and does affect the working efficiency during winters, especially in the months of January and February when the city usually experiences heavy snowfall, and also because of congestion and housing problem for the employees, the Board was later shifted to Dharamshala. Dharamshala is District and Divisional Headquarters of Kangra District and Revenue Division of the State.

Status and Composition of the Board

All the Boards, in conduct and functioning are autonomous and independent bodies though they form part of the respective State Departments of Education and run under their control. Executive head of the Board is the Chairman. In West Bengal, the executive heads of all the four Boards are called Presidents and in Andhra Board, they are designated as Directors of Government Examination.

The composition as stipulated in Acts of the Boards is: Chairman, Vice Chairman, Ex-officio member, Elected member, and Nominated members.

It was found that out of the seven Boards: (1) none of the Boards has a Vice-Chairman's post; rather all have secretary's post. (2) The term of the Chairman/President is for three years, which can be extended by one more term. HPSEB is such an example. The Chairman of the HPSEB has been given an extension of one more term.

Function of the Board

All the Boards carry out functions according to the respective state Acts. Some common functions are:

- To frame conditions for recognition of high and higher secondary schools and the qualifications of the teaching staff;
- To appoint committees of experts to advise on the syllabi for the different courses of study;
- To frame courses of study on the recommendations of expert committees;
- To draw up panels of question paper setters, chief examines and assistant examiners;
- To frame rules prescribing the minimum conditions for selection of examiners, assistant examiners and other rules for allied work;
- To conduct examinations as required by the regulations;
- To issue certificates to successful candidates; and
- Generally to advise the Director of Education when required, on all matters pertaining to secondary education.

Inspection of Schools

Generally, the department of public instruction or Directorate of Education does inspection of schools. But sometimes education authorities in collaboration with the Board office inspect the schools to see that academic work goes on as per syllabi, so that there is no deception in the functioning of the schools.

In HP, the Board has the power to grant affiliation to private schools, on the basis that the schools meet the standard requirement of building, teaching staff, equipment and other educational facilities. Thus the control and check on private schools lies in the hands of HPSEB. Out of the1700-affiliated private schools, 87 were personally visited last year by present Chairman of the Board. In 66 of these private schools flaws were found and notices issued to them. Some school principals give false lists of teachers whom they never appoint them. To check this malpractice, photographs of teachers have to be furnished to the Board. In addition, every school has to submit the certificate of firefighting from competent safety authorities.

Curriculum Development

The State Boards are required to design suitable curricula and syllabi for different stages of education as per guidelines prescribed by NCERT. The NCERT is a nodal agency for providing guidelines for the authorities in the different states in their curriculum framing exercise. The states have adopted suggestions with modifications here and there.

This function differs from state to state. Out of the four Boards, West Bengal and Madhya Pradesh Board design and prescribe their own curriculum, according to the guidelines supplied by NCERT. Himachal Pradesh on the other hand, at the secondary level adopts NCERT curriculum with minor modification. However at senior secondary level, it adopts NCERT's syllabus for science stream, to help students of the hilly state to join the national mainstream.

In Andhra Pradesh curriculum development function is with the State Council of Educational Research and Training. Special emphasis has been laid on curriculum aspects as education towards active citizenship and human rights, environmental issues, universal values, etc. Teaching materials have been developed in these areas also.

In West Bengal out of the four Boards, WBBSE and WBCHSE design and prescribe their own curriculum. The responsibility of publishing books have been given by WBBSE and WBCHSE to private publishers, with the conditions that price, number of pages pictures, charts, lines on one page, paper quality, size of the books, etc. will be fixed by the Board. Private publishers cannot increase the number of pages than those fixed. The reason for fixed number of pages is because many publishing houses are in the habit of violating the rules and norms prescribed by the Board. In many cases volume of a book becomes the cause of panic for the students, as the prescribed syllabus is artificially and unnecessarily made to appear much heavier than it actually is. Also difference in norms of information and data presentation in different books create confusion among the students. The Boards also control the price of the textbooks. The books prescribed by the Boards are not very costly; their price ranges between Rs. 18 to 27 per book. WBBSE and WBCHSE also keep control on quality of the book while publishing school's textbooks. The Boards ask publishers to use four colour cover with DTP printing and maplitho paper for its textbooks.

The West Bengal Board of Madrasah Education (WBBME) introduced re-oriented syllabus and curriculum as prescribed by

WBBSE and WBCHSE, thus establishing parity with WBBSE and WBCHSE.

Vocational Education

In accordance with the priority accorded to vocational education in the NPE, 1986, a centrally sponsored scheme of vocationalisation of secondary education was started in 1988. The main objectives are to provide diversification of educational opportunities so as to enhance individual employability, reduce the mismatch between demand and supply of skilled manpower and to provide an alternative for those pursuing higher education.

The Centrally sponsored scheme of pre-vocational secondary stage was launched in 1993-94 with the objective of imparting training in simple marketable skills to students of Classes IX and X. As the secondary level is a terminal stage of mass education, the core subject therefore is compulsory for all students in all the Boards. However, there are a large number of students who leave school after secondary stage and join the world of work as unskilled labour or manage some kind of self-employment. To meet their requirement pre-vocational courses have been included in WBBSE and BSEAP. But these courses are optional and additional than the core subjects. In WBBSE, the marks a student scores in the additional subject, are reduced by 34 marks, and the rest are added in the total marks of the student, scored in the secondary school examination.

In BSEAP the vocational courses are called 'Life Skills Subjects'. According to the need of the regions certain trades have been introduced in some schools as of 'Life Skills Subjects'. At present there are 15 trades. The students have choice to select one or two trades from the list of the trades available in that region. The students have to appear in the examination for the academic courses along with the vocational course. The students who opt for vocational courses are given two certificates, i.e., one in academic and other in vocational course. While developing the curriculum for vocational education, the varying needs of not only the girls, SC/ST and physically handicapped persons but also the communities living in rural, urban and different geographical areas are taken into consideration and the number of courses developed, thereby making the choice available to the students to select the vocation as per their select needs and requirements.

BSEMP is planning to introduce pre-vocational courses at secondary level. For this purpose, the scheme is going to be introduced on experimental basis in certain schools. In HPBSE, at the secondary level, no initiative had yet been taken by the Board to introduce vocational courses.

At the senior secondary level, since the colonial period various commissions and committees have been suggesting introduction of vocational courses at senior secondary levels. All the Boards had introduced vocational courses, but a very few students opt for these courses. According to Kothari Commission enrolment in vocational courses should be 50 per cent at the higher secondary level. In WBCHSE participation level of students in vocational courses was only.64 per cent during 2002-03. HPBSE at senior secondary level had recently identified relevant areas and accordingly appropriate curriculum has been designed. These courses have been blended with work education. The courses introduced were food processing, aquaculture, trance agency operations, computer network, consumer electronics, riverine and reservoir fisheries, hospitality, industry and business, food packaging, etc. BSEMP has introduced 31 trades. The curriculum is prepared by SCERT. The curriculum committee of the Board approves it. Then the curriculum is included in the syllabus of the Board examination.

Examination

Mapping of the Evaluation Journey

All the Boards do mapping of evaluation journey:

- Students submit answer sheets to the invigilator at the exam centre. Centre superintendent supervises the sealing of the papers;
- Sealed answer sheets are dispatched to the Board;
- In the Board, original roll numbers are removed and fictitious code numbers are given to conceal identity of students or stickers are pasted on the original roll numbers;
- The answer sheets then are sent to evaluation centres. Evaluations are done by a marking scheme decided by the subject experts;
- On the first day, evaluators clear any doubts they may have, regarding minute details in the marking scheme, with the head examiners or nodal supervisor;

- The answer sheets are also seen by an additional examiner, head examiner and the nodal chief supervisor at the evaluation center;
- Once evaluation deadlines are met, the answer sheets are then sent back to the Board; and
- Then result analysis and processing is done.

Re-evaluation/Revaluation Facility

In BSEMP, re-checking of marks can be opted by students, who are not satisfied by their marks. The scrutiny committee verifies the marks and if any question or a part of question is found unvalued, it gets valued. In the event of change in result or no change in the result, whatever may be the case, it is communicated to the student within a month. If a student's total in marks increases and the result of the candidate changes, then the fee deposited by him is refunded. Second, if a failed candidate comes in the category of passed candidate, not only the fee deposited by the candidate is refunded but also an amount of Rs. 500 is also paid to the student by the Board. However, re-evaluation of papers is not done.

In WBBSE and WBCHSE, re-evaluation of answer scripts is done in two ways: Post Publication Review, and Post Publication Scrutiny.

HPBSE permits re-evaluation and re-checking of answer books. Recently, to have transparency in the paper checking a reform has been introduced by the Board, that is the answer scripts are shown to the student concerned.

Supplementary Examination

In addition to the annual examination Boards also conduct supplementary exams.

HPBSE, from 2001 onwards, gives two chances (March and September) to students to appear in the supplementary examination. Sometimes at the discretion of the Chairman, students who are not able to clear supplementary exam in two chances, also get a third chance, known as 'golden chance'.

Andhra Pradesh and Madhya Pradesh Boards give only one chance to appear in the supplementary exams. Within a month after declaration of student's final exam, supplementary exam is conducted and results are declared within 10 days, so that students may save one year.

Composite Curriculum

In West Bengal the examinations are conducted on the basis of composite units taught in Classes XI and XII for Higher Secondary, while in other states in most of the cases, the final examinations are held covering the topics meant for Class XII only.

Pattern of Question Paper

In BSEMP, WBBSE and HPBSE the format of question papers for secondary and senior secondary examinations have been changed. Now the question papers contain five types of questions—very short answer questions, short answer questions, medium, and long answer/ essay type questions. The total number of questions of every kind is fixed. The places where internal options have to be put are demarcated. The marking scheme is also provided with not only the number of questions but also with the answer contents.

Multi-Set Question Paper Method

Up to mid 1990s generally most of the Boards were using a single paper scheme. Simultaneously, however, they increased the number of questions with more internal options. This practice still prevails in BSEAP, in order that all levels of students, such as backward, average, intelligent, etc., are able to answer the questions. But now, in most of the Boards, care is taken to include questions from all the three areas, i.e., knowledge, comprehensive, and application of skill. Also these Boards are providing multi-set question papers. For this purpose subject-wise content analysis is made and priorities of every subject are decided by the subject committee. Then Boards develop a blueprint of every question paper. In this technique multiple-choice questions are avoided. Three sets of all the papers with common questions are prepared.

Paper Setter

In all the Boards, experienced teachers set the question papers. For each subject, 3 sets of question paper are set. Then the question papers are sent to moderators.

Non-detention system

In BSEAP, non-detention system has been introduced except for

Classes VII and X. and evaluation procedure has been strengthened by continuous and comprehensive evaluation in all the classes.

Grace Marks

In BSEMP, maximum 5 grace marks may be given in one subject or five subjects. The grace marks are not added in the total marks defined by the students in that specific subject. Only 'by grace' is stated in front of such subject or subjects.

In WBBSE, if a candidate fails to pass in one compulsory subject by not more than 5 per cent marks, he/she shall be given credit by transfer of marks from the highest marks scored by him or her in a compulsory subject to make up the deficiency in the subject in which he/she fails.

Continuous and Comprehensive Evaluation

In HPBSE, BSEMP, WBBSE, WBCHSE and WBBME, except secondary and senior secondary classes, continuous and comprehensive evaluation is carried out in all the classes. To maintain quality of education, final assessment is made on the basis of monthly unit tests and periodical examinations such as quarterly, half-yearly and annual examinations.

In BSEAP, except Classes VII and X apart from academic performance personal and social qualities, interest-based activities, observation of student's work in the library, laboratory, physical health activities in the playground, in the school, particularly in different activities in the school, are assessed and non-scholastic achievement certificate is given to the students along with academic performance.

In WBBSE, till the mid 1990's Work Education, Physical Education, Social Service were considered as compulsory papers for the final examination. Form 1996, this group of papers has been shifted to the list of additional optional subjects. The Board found it difficult to arrange proper evaluation of these non-scholastics subjects.

Number of Chances Given for Clearing a Public Examination

In BSEAP and HPBSE, there are no limits for the number of attempts to appear for the Board examinations.

In BSEMP, students are given two chances, i.e., the annual and the supplementary to clear the examination. If a student, declared eligible to appear in a supplementary examination, fails there too, he may appear as a private candidate subsequently; two more chances are given to him. If he fails in both of them, he may be entertained as student of correspondence course by the Board.

Checking Unfair Means in Examinations

All the Boards are taking strict actions to check unfair means in the examinations. Following the 'Acts' they have constituted unfair mean committees. The committee decides the cases of unfair means. In HPBSE to create awareness about the evil effects of copying, the students of all schools, before they take their examination, are administrated an oath of sincerity and probity so that they could desist from indulging in this evil practice at least on moral grounds. Though the Boards are taking strict measures to stop the means of copying in examination, still this practice continues in schools.

In WBBSE and WBCHSE, unfair means of cases are very few. In BSEMP, in spite of all efforts in some of the border districts of Madhya Pradesh and in interior areas of schools, this practice still continues. Therefore, close cooperation is taken from the district administration. During examination time, flying squads of the Board and district officials are constituted for surprise checks. The BSEMP was facing the problem of use of unfair means, even after the completion of the examination. Miscreants change inner pages of answer copies. To counter-check this problem, the Board has changed the pattern of answer books since 2004 and has introduced thread-stitching copyies. Secondly, after completion of examination time, the answer books are deposited at the nearest police station everyday. These are finally picked up at the end of all examinations.

In BSEMP, HPBSE and BSEAP, to maintain secrecy of the identity of the candidates appeared in the examinations, special 'stickers' are pasted on the roll numbers and dummy codes are given to each answer book. These 'stickers' are removed only after the answer books are evaluated. On the other hand, in WBBSE and WBCHSE, to hide the identity of students in the public examinations, roll numbers given to students were of special category. The roll number is of 10 digits. First three digits show district code, next three points to institute/school, next two digits are about the stream of students, and the last two digits tell about the gender of the student. Every year the code of these digits are changed to maintain secrecy.

Financial Management

BSEMP, HPBSE, WBBSE and WBCHSE are self-sufficient Boards. No grants are taken from the government. They generate their own resources. On the other hand, BSEAP is fully supported by the Government. BSEMP is able to generate surplus income. Out of the surplus income meritorious students are given scholarships and in addition, in the absence of a pension scheme, the Board has started giving this benefit from the earning of the Board to its employees.

Information Technology Courses

The subject of Information Technology (IT) has been introduced at the senior secondary level in HPBSE, BSEMP and WBBSE. In HPBSE at the senior secondary level the schools running IT courses are provided with Internet connections and also magazines related to the field of IT are subscribed. In Madhya Pradesh Board, two new subjects, i.e., Business Mathematics, and Computer Applications have been added to the Humanities and Commerce group at the senior secondary stage.

In BSEMP, the subject of Computer Application has been introduced in commerce group.

WBBSE has introduced Computer Education as an optional subject for Classes IX and X. Computer Application as an additional subject has been introduced in schools. The Board also conducts computer literacy programmes.

Journal Published

All the Boards publish monthly or quarterly journals, which exclusively print essays on current problems of education in India, and directives, and notifications issued by the Board from time to time. Hence, the journals are an effective bridge between schools and Boards, because these link schools situated in the remotest areas of the state with the office of the Boards at the headquarters. The articles published help to enhance quality of secondary education.

Computerisation of Examination Results

All the Boards have completely computerised the examination results. But none have their own computer centres. Feeding of examination data as well as analysis of results is outsourced by all the Boards.

The WBCHSE claims that it has created precedence in India by issuing mark sheets and certificates on the same day as of the declaration of the result.

Declaration of Results

All the Boards publish public examination results through various mediums, like website of the Board, E-mail, Lokmitra Suchna Kendra, IBRS telephone facility, official gazettes, and through other private telecom companies like IDEA, Airtel, Hutch, BSNL etc. These companies can be approached through SMS.

Research Wing

None of the Boards has a Research Wing. The research helps in enhancing the quality of education by brining change in the functioning of the system, curriculum and syllabus.

Merit List

All the Boards acknowledge best students in the Boards' examinations. They publish their names, photographs in the newspapers or in school magazines. In West Bengal in all the Boards, if a candidate obtains 80 per cent marks in a subject, he/she is awarded 'Letter' in the subject and the award is indicated in the mark sheet. If a candidate obtains 75 per cent marks in the aggregate, he/she is declared to have passed with 'Star', which is indicated in the mark sheet.

But while acknowledging meritorious students, hardly any Board takes care of non-scholastic achievement.

Conclusions

Quality has become an important issue and concern in secondary education because of several reasons. One, expansion of elementary education due to government's commitment for universalisation of elementary education has increased the demand for secondary education. Second, due to globalisation and global competitiveness, India's chance of coming within the competitive range is dependent upon the quality of her manpower. As secondary education is a terminal stage of education, one can consider secondary education as the baseline for the workforce. The growing private tuitions and coaching market is a best example of demand for quality education. (West Bengal's example can be cited. At the higher secondary level, the students' attendance is very low and the main cause behind all this is that a lot of emphasis is being placed on private tuitions.) Therefore secondary education is going to occupy the centre stage of education and national development in the coming years.

Quality of education generally depends upon three indicators: Curriculum, Teaching-Learning Process and Examination Process. In all the schools, the curriculum is guided by NCERT by the National Curriculum Framework and translated into action strategies through textbooks designed by NCERT as well as the State Textbook Boards. An effort in curriculum development needs to respond to the up-coming challenges: In the globalised world, the curriculum framework must have international reference. Besides, as India is dominantly multi-cultural society, the curriculum should focus on multi-cultural curriculum. The efforts in curriculum development need to respond to these challenges. The NCERTs National Curriculum Framework offers provision for regional and local contents. But in reality, it hardly happens. States either accept NCERT's national framework, and the syllabus and textbooks are developed on this basis, or reject completely and go on their own. For example three-language formula is not accepted by all the states in the form suggested by the NCERT. While Tamil Nadu follows a two-language policy, in West Bengal the third language is taught only in Classes VII and VIII. But never before did the states find any occasion to basically differ with the national framework as in its latest version that seeks to include 'education about religions' in school curriculum. This proposition has created a sharp division among states. There are few states that prepare their own curriculum and textbooks. In West Bengal, the major guidelines contained in the national pattern are duly considered, but a broad-based democratic process is followed in finalising the courses. The challenge is to develop a consensus and a mechanism for creating a judicious mixture of national, regional and local contents. In a multi–cultural society a common syllabus and a set of common textbooks have limited applicability. Need is to develop or design competency-based education.

Second indicator of quality in school education is instructional strategy or teaching-learning process. As far as teaching-learning process is concerned, teachers still believe in lecture method. They teach mostly through lecture method. Therefore, teachers need to be trained to use Information Technology related equipments in the classroom process.

Third indicator of quality is evaluation or examination process. The purpose of examination is to discover whether students have assimilated the knowledge and skills required by the curriculum and whether they have reached an adequate level of maturity in line with the goals of secondary schools. But over the years examination process has deviated from its path and it has become the mean to get certification for entry into higher education. In this context of conducting school examination and issuing certificates, Board of Secondary Education has its importance. Therefore, a significant area for consideration in secondary education is the role of Boards in achieving the quality of Secondary education. The success of the Boards depends upon how much they cope with management of change to maintain quality in education.

Recommendations

- Secondary Education needs to be reached to large section of society. Therefore Boards have to think in terms of universalisation of secondary education.
- The Boards need to advise the State Government on all matters relating to secondary education. In addition laying down the general policy for development of secondary education, instead of only envisaging on examinations and related activities.
- There is a need to modernize the Education Boards through information technology enabled system.
- Strengthen research and development cell. The research would provide feedback to the Board to improve school administration and functioning of the Board.
- The Boards need to widen the sphere of their operations and increasingly support schools in undertaking innovative activities and in offering high quality education.
- The Boards should be given a statutory status with substantial autonomy followed by accountability, which will enable them to function as key institutions for improving the quality of school education.
- In the globalise era national boundaries are weakening; the Boards have to think regarding curriculum not only in the context of national level but also from the point of view of international level.
- Industries, science laboratories, service sectors need to be

actively involved in curriculum design and updating. The life period of curriculum is to be shorter than the present and periodical or annual reviews may be required to meet the challenges of the society.

- The curriculum has to accommodate any number of basic disciplines and has to provide learner-friendly inputs. The learner would have the freedom and choice to select his own discipline.
- Strong coordination between with Directorates and the Boards needs to be developed for monitoring school education. Examination is a sub-system of the of formal education system to evaluate academic programmes. But how academic program takes place in the classroom is hardly taken care of by the Boards.
- Standards in curriculum and evaluation of students should be comparable among all the State Education Boards.
- Need for flexibility in the choice of subjects of studies. Let students decide what subject they want to learn.
- Need for change in the mechanisms of examination. Examination should be subordinate to teaching and it should follow the curriculum. Unfortunately, examinations dictate the curriculum and teaching is subordinate to examination. Therefore need of reform in the examination system.
- Apart from academic performance, non-scholastics subjects should be given weightage at the secondary school certificate exam.
- The flexibility in number of attempts to appear for the Board's examination may be increased to reduce stress on students.
- The curriculum needs to be evaluated periodically. The curriculum development should be on the basis of national level framework and local area needs. The stress should be given on vocational programmes.
- Generate vocation awareness programme at the primary and upper primary level.
- Need is to increase enrolment in vocational course by strengthening the course.
- System of co-ordination with industries, universities, higher education institutions, etc. may be developed.
- Need to improve pre-evaluation checks rather than leaving scope for re-evaluation.

- Need of central evaluation to ensure uniformity and objectivity in marking answer scripts for brining about uniformity.
- Analysis of subject-wise results of individual schools, and based on the definitions detected the concerned school, are cautioned to improve upon the teaching programme of the subject in which poor performance of students needs to be observed.
- Need of training to principals, teachers, paper setters, moderators, and evaluators.
- Need for training programmes of examiners in different subjects. The purpose is to make the examiners conversant with the modern trends in examination and evaluation system.
- To minimize unfair means, strict supervisors should be appointed. Capability should be the only criteria for appointment of supervisors and not the seniority.
- Malpractices and adoption of unfair means in examination hall are now becoming a headache for most of the Boards. It is seen that the students become the victim, but the erring teachers and others are spared. Therefore exemplary punishment should be meted out to the erring teachers and other who promote malpractice.
- The different Sate Boards of Education adopt different measures to meet the challenge of use of unfair means in the various public examinations. Some Boards have adopted measures like enactment of law by state assemblies. There is a need to sit down and exchange experience regularly on issues like leakage of question papers, mass copying etc. The Boards can discuss their own processes, mistakes and how they have overcome in spite of their inadequacies.
- The State Boards should encourage schools to optimise the academic resources available and explore the possibilities of utilising alternative academic resources of parents and community at large.
- The organisation spends resources according to their priority areas. Expenditure of the Boards shows that expenditure activities are either made on staff salaries, examination related activities or non-recurring activities like change of vehicle or construction of building. Hardly resources are spent on academic or research activities. The need of the

hour is: Boards should spend on academic and research activities.

- At present examination is loosing acceptability. Every employer or institutions of higher education are taking their own selection tests. One of the significant innovative schemes in the field of evaluation is Continuous and Comprehensive Evaluation (CCE). The purpose of the scheme is to widen the area of evaluation to cover the total personality of the child. This includes all the areas of assessment, which need to be tested through the Board's examination.
- To popularise CCE and for its implementation, articles, papers and research studies on this scheme need to be given preference in the 'Board's Journal'. In addition commendable efforts of selected institutions should be published in the Journal.
- The mechanism of recognition of schools by the state government/Board should be strictly followed for both types of schools: government and private.
- Need to have E-connectivity for having better network between the schools and the Board. In Hilly states the problem of physical barrier will thus be overcome.

Bibliography

Aggarwal, Yash and Kusum K. Premi. Reforming School Education: Issues in Policy Planning and Implementation. (Edited), NIEPA, 1998.

Annual Budgets, Board of Secondary Education, Bhopal, Madhya Pradesh, 2000, 2001, 2002, 2003, 2004.

Annual Reports, Department of School Education, Bikash Bhavan, Kolkata, 1998-99, 1999-2000, 2000-2001, 2001-2002, 2002-2003.

Annual Reports, Himachal Pradesh School Education Board, Dharamsala, 1998, 1999, 2000, 2001, 2002, 2003.

Baltimore, MD, State Board of Education. http://www.Mdarchives.state.md.us/msa/mdmanual/13 sdoe/html/13 agen.html

Grading in Public Examination, CBSE 2000.

Examination Reform in India COBSE.

Dong-Seop, J. The Education System in Korea. http:/aped.snu.ac.in

Education–The German Way. http://www.german-way.com

Examination Administration, Academic Affairs: Assessment Policy and Practice. wwvv.rgu.acak/subj/aas/exams.htm

Examination Reforms: A Report of the Regional Seminar, Organised by Assam Higher Secondary Education Council, Guwahati in Collaboration with COBSE, Delhi, 1997.

France Educational System. http:/www.discoverfrance.net

Garkhar, B.B., Basics of Good School, *Hindustan Times, Nov. 27, 2004,* West Delhi.

Hanushek E.A. and Raymond M.E., Improving Educational Quality: How Best to Evaluate Our Schools? Paper presented for *Education in the 21st Century: Meeting the Challenges of a Changing World*, Federal Reserve Bank, 2002.

India, Ministry of Education, Government of India, Report of the Education Commission, 1964-66.

Indian State Board of Education. www.Kindstart.com/education day Carechild/state boards departments of education/statelistings.html

Japanese Education System. http://www.japan-guide.com

Journal *Him Lok*: Himachal Pradesh School Education Board, Dharamshala; 1995, 1999, 2000.

Journal *Parikshak*: Board of Secondary Education, MP; 2000, 2001, 2002, 2003, 2004.

Khandelwal, B.P., Some Futuristic Paradigms for Boards of School Education. (mimeo.), NIEPA, 2003

Majumdar Tapas, An Education Commission Reports, *Economic and Political Weekly*, May 8, 1993.

Management of Recognised Non-government Institutions (Aided and Unaided Rules, 1969), as amended up to 1984, WBBSE.

Mills P., Developing Leadership Within: Thinking About the Future of the State Education Department. Report of the State Board of Regents, New York (2001). www.nysed.gov/comm/regol04a.htm

Mukhopadhyay M. & Manju Narula, Secondary Education – The Challenges Ahead (edited), NIEPA, 2002.

Mukhopadhyay M. & Parhar Madhu. Open and Distance Education. New Delhi, Jawahar Publishers, 1997.

Mukhopadhyay, Sudesh, Enhancing the Academic Role of Boards of School Education. (edited), NIEPA, 2002.

National Policy on Education, 1986, Ministry of Human Resource Development, Government of India.

News Bulletin; Himachal Pradesh Board, May-June 2001.

NCERT, Sixth All India Survey, New Delhi, 1995.

Organisation of the Examination Session. www.meq. gouv.qc.ca/sanction/epreuv_a. uni/partie l.htm

Organisational Set-up, Management of CBSE, www.cbseindia.org/manage-1org.htm.

Paramaswaram, E.G., Examination, Evaluation 'n' Assessment; Education Tracks, February, 2002.

Programme of Action, 1992, Ministry of Human Resource Development, Government of India.

Quality Improvement in Madrasah Planning and Management: Role of the Head of Madrasah, Training Guide, WBBME, Kolkata.

Remodeling of School Education Boards: Report of the Task Force on the Role & Status of Boards of Secondary Education, MHRD, New Delhi, 1997.

Report of Board of High School and Intermediate Education, UP, Tata Consultancy Services, 1997.

Report of the Education Commission (Ashok Mitra), August 1992, Government of West Bengal.

Report of West Bengal: Since Independence State Studies in School Education, SCERT, West Bengal, 2002.

Secondary Education Commission, (1952-53), Ministry of Education, Government of India.

Secondary School Examination systems in Countries in the SEAMEO Region, http://www.seameo.org

Sharma, K.D., Credibility of Examinations, *Journal of Indian Education*, August, 1995.

Sharma, O.P., *Administration Boards in India,* Ashish Publishing House, New Delhi, 1991.

Singh, Amrik, Combining Moral Commitment with Pragmatism: Ashok Mitra Commission on Education, *Economic and Political Weekly*, July 17-24, 1993.

Singh, H.S., History of Examination Reforms in India, NCERT, 2003.

Singhal R.P., The New Examination System. http://shikshanic.nic.in

Structure of Education in Iceland. http://www.eroeducation.net.

Sujatha K. Distance Education at Secondary Level in India, National Open School, UNESCO, IIEP, 2002.

Tata Consultancy Services. Organisation Structure Study, Board of High School and Intermediate Education, UP, 1997.

The Finnish Matriculation Examination Board, 1998.

The Kolkata Gazette, WB/SC-247, 2001.

The National Association of State Boards of Education (NASBE). www.nabe.Org/profilebody/html

UK School Education Structure and Curriculum—Education and Training. British Council, http://www.britishcouncil.org

United States of America—Education System, http://www.use.edu/dept/education

University Education Commission, 1948-49. Ministry of Education, Government of India, 1950.

Using Grades for Admissions, NCERT, 2001.

Villanueva C.L., Technology in Education: Meeting Future Challenges, Reforming Learning, Curriculum and Pedagogy: Innovative Vision for the New Century, Bangkok, Thailand, 1999.

West Bengal Act V of 1963; WBBSE, Calcutta.

Index